Passport to Cambridge
First Certificate

Teacher's Book

Peter Dainty

First published 1990
Reprinted 1991, 1992, 1993

Published by MACMILLAN PUBLISHERS LTD
London and Basingstoke

ISBN 0 – 333 – 53388 – 7

Printed in Hong Kong

A CIP catalogue record for this book is available from the British Library

Produced by AMR

Contents

UNIT	PHOTOGRAPH	TEXTS	GRAMMAR	VOCABULARY	COMMUNICATIVE ACTIVITIES	PHRASAL VERBS
1	'The Italian Restaurant' (1)	'Paul's pie in the sky' (2) Boeing advert (3)	prepositions of time (7) plurals (8) question words + *ever* (9) *make* and *do* (10)	ladybird (4)	pronunciation (5) the definite article (6)	study skills (11) cartoon (12)
2	'The Gesture' (1)	'What do Puerto Ricans do . . .?' (3) Dishwash electric advert (6)	*so/such/such a(n)* (7) emphatic use of *too* (8) *some/any* (9) *get* (11)	multiple choice (2) ladybird (5) ladybird (10) differences (12)	writing letters (4) *get* (11)	cartoon (13)
3	'The Girls' School' (1)	'Balloony Branson's UFO prank backfires' (3)	question tags (5) present simple and continuous (6)	multiple choice (2)	Voyager 2 (4) life at the age 11–16 (7) homophones (8) the answerphone (9)	cartoon (10)
4	'The Couple' (1)	'The yuppie conmen trick homehunters' (3)	*have* (4) infinitives (5) *enough* (6)	multiple choice (2) ladybird (8) differences (9)	*have* (4) choosing a suitable reply (7)	cartoon (10)
5	'The Market' (1)	'Dolphins save surf boy . . .' (3) Access advert (4)	gerunds (5) temporals & conditionals (6) reported speech (7) present perfect & simple past (8) *must/should/ought* (10)	multiple choice (2)	The lion (9) The children's charter (10)	*call* (11) cartoon (12)
6	'The Currency Traders' (1)	'Do you eat too much?' (3)	conditionals (4) comparatives (6) the apostrophe (7) simple past & past perfect (8) superlatives (9)	multiple choice (2)	conditionals (4) Children and the law (5)	cartoon (10)
7	'The Round Table' (1)	Midland Care Card advert (3) 'New nation of Eskimos . . .' (5) Frank Pepperton story (5)	adverbs of frequency (6) *must/might/can't be* (7) *wish* (8) *used* (9)	multiple choice (2)	Charities (4) the Totally Truthful Travel Company (6) five friends (7) 'I wish . . .' (8)	cartoon (10)
8	'The boy and the elephant' (1)	'Boy, 7, yanks out five teeth . . .' (3)	active & passive (7) *over-/under-* (8)	multiple choice (2) ladybird (5)	The tooth fairy (4) The advertising game (6)	cartoon/text (9)

UNIT	PHOTOGRAPH	TEXTS	GRAMMAR	VOCABULARY	COMMUNICATIVE ACTIVITIES	PHRASAL VERBS
9	'Mist' (1)	'Abominable snowstorm grinds Britain to a halt' (3)	*have something done* (4) *else* (6) *raise/rise* (7)	multiple choice (2) differences (5)	Size (8)	cartoon/text (9)
10	'The Toy Stall' (1)	'Found among the milk bottles . . .' (3)	countable & uncountable nouns (4) *lay* and *lie* (5) prepositions (6) *up* (7) *less/free* (10)	multiple choice (2) ladybird (12)	The touts (8) The horse race (9) Describing & drawing (12)	Writing exercise (11) cartoon/text (13)
11	'The Chinese School' (1)	'Sorry darling, I just popped out . . .' (3) 'Starting school can be child's play' (7)		multiple choice (2) My uncle Theodore (5) word families (8)	Flags (4) The forest game (6) Paper 2 essay (10)	*take* (9) cartoon/text (11)
12	'The London Marathon' (1)	Greenpeace brochure (3) 'One fast woman' (5)		multiple choice (2) DIY blank filling (4)	Paper 2 essay (6) The wedding (7) Wedding anniversaries (8) pronunciation (9)	cartoon/text (10)
13	'The Skydivers' (1)	'Man-made bee leads dance of the hive' (3) 'Some people do, and some people don't (5)		multiple choice (2) blank filling (9) word families (10)	groups of 5 words (4) Sign language (6) Agatha Christie (7) The radio play (8) questionnaire (9)	*keep* (11) cartoon/text (13)
14	'Yawning' (1)	Halifax advert (4)		multiple choice (2) Paper 3 (6)	Radio news bulletin (3) A cookery class (3) At the garage (3) Paper 2 (5) Papers 4 & 5 (6)	*put* (7) cartoon/text (8)
15	'The Wedding' (1)	Three jokes (7)		multiple choice (2) differences (4) linking the letters (6)	East Lather Street (3) 'Raise your hand' (5)	cartoon (8)
Practice Test						

THE EXAM

Since its modest beginnings in 1939, the Cambridge First Certificate (once known as the Lower Cambridge) has become the standard international test of English as a Foreign Language at a higher intermediate level.

The exam is now held twice a year (in June and December) at 400 centres in the United Kingdom and 250 centres abroad. You can take 'FC' in over sixty countries, from Austria to Zimbabwe, and the qualification is recognised by governments, universities and companies all over the world.

There are five separate papers, spread over two days, which each test a different language skill: reading, writing, grammar, listening and speaking.

Paper 1 – Reading Comprehension (One hour. 40 marks)

Twenty-five multiple choice vocabulary questions.

Fifteen multiple choice reading comprehension questions
(based on three different texts).

Paper 2 – Essay Writing (One and a half hours. 40 marks)

Two essays from a range of five topics.
(Each essay must be between 120 and 180 words long.)

Paper 3 – Use of English (Two hours. 40 marks)

Part A – Grammar

A blank filling exercise

Grammar transformations

A 50/50 dialogue

Word families

Phrasal verb questions.

Part B – Directed Writing

Four paragraphs of approximately 50 words each
(based on the reworking of given material).

Paper 4 – Listening Comprehension (30 minutes. 20 marks)

Three (sometimes four) passages with follow-up questions in a variety of
formats such as: blank filling
multiple choice
true or false.

Paper 5 – Interview (approx. 20 minutes. 40 marks)

Either one-to-one or in a group.

You will be asked to: describe a photograph
summarise and interpret a passage
participate in an open-ended discussion
or   discuss one of the three set books.

UCLES PUBLICATIONS

First Certificate is one of a number of exams organised by the University of Cambridge Local Examinations Syndicate and if you are teaching 'FC' for the first time, it's a good idea to contact UCLES and ask about the various exam-related materials they publish.

In the first instance write to:

> The Examinations Secretary
> University of Cambridge Local Examinations Syndicate
> 1 Hills Road
> Cambridge
> CB1 2BU
> England

and ask for a Publications Order Form. Then I would suggest you send off for some or all of the following publications:

a *English as a Foreign Language* This is essential reading for anyone teaching a Cambridge exam class. It contains detailed information about the syllabus, structure and marking schemes of all the UCLES exams: First Certificate, Proficiency, The Diploma of English Studies, The Preliminary English Test, The Certificate in English for International Communication, The Cambridge Examination in English for Language Teachers etc.

b The *Exam Regulations* (which are published two years in advance) include details of which three set books have been set for a particular year.

c The *Exam Survey* gives details of the results for the previous year.

d List of Centres (updated every six months).

e Question Papers for previous exams are available as individual copies, as group sets or as five complete papers in a book.

PASSPORT TO FIRST CERTIFICATE

The *Passport to Cambridge First Certificate* series includes:

- a main course book
- a free-standing workbook, *Personal Passport*, which contains advice about exam techniques as well as extensive practice material for Papers 1, 2 and 3.
- a teacher's book
- a cassette featuring the 34 listening exercises.

The main course book has ten basic elements.

1 Photographs

Each chapter begins with a photograph and a series of exam style follow-up questions. The first two or three questions are very general ('Where was the photograph taken?' 'What can you see in the picture?' etc.); the next two or three are more specific ('What instruments are being played?' 'Describe the conductor,' etc.); and then there are questions about related themes ('Do you like music?' 'Who is your favourite composer?' etc.).

2 Multiple choice vocabulary exercises

These are given in the same format as Section A of Paper 1.

3 Reading comprehension texts

These have been taken from a wide range of contemporary primary source materials – newspapers, magazines, leaflets, novels, advertisements – and are accompanied by follow-up questions on vocabulary, comprehension and phrasal verbs.

4 Grammar

In the first ten units of the book, there are some 45 formal grammar exercises presented in a three-tier format of Example-Explanation-Exercise.

These and other grammar points are then tested in the exam style exercises of units 11 to 15.

Additional information is given in the comprehensive grammar reference section at the back of the book which, among other things, explains the various tenses and common uses of common verbs.

5 Writing

There are four kinds of writing exercise:

a summaries – with a range of tasks designed to build student confidence and bridge the gap between making a sentence and writing a 180–word free-form essay.

b directed writing exercises – based on primary source material such as the Halifax Building Society's 'Guide To Buying A House' and the article from *Cosmopolitan* magazine.

c composition practice

d double translation exercises – where the student translates a text into his or her mother tongue and then, some time later, translates that second text back into English.

6 Blank filling

Five exam format exercises complementing the extensive cloze test material found in *Personal Passport*.

7 Listening

Thirty-four different pieces, with particular emphasis on the multiple choice comprehension, true/false and gap filling exercises found in the exam.

8 Discrete

'Ladybird', 'differences', 'collocations' etc. – free-standing exercises that can be done as pair, group or class work.

9 Pair and Group work

A wide range of communicative and creative exercises.

10 The phrasal verb story

A cartoon serial that introduces 325 of the phrasal and prepositional verb forms that students find so difficult.

The self-study workbook, *Personal Passport*, includes:

- advice on how to prepare for First Certificate
- exam tips for each of the five papers
- ten cloze exercises with a detailed analysis of the grammar points raised
- exercises on collocations and ladybird words
- a full list of answers.

METHODS

There is no single correct way to use any material, and only the individual teacher can decide how to adapt a book for the particular needs of his or her particular class. However, I do think there are some general points that are worth making.

a Whenever possible, have a conversation with the class. Ask students to define words, give examples, ask questions and raise related issues. Talk *with* the group, not *at* it.

b When there's a lot of detailed, technical information in the book, use the board summary technique.

c Ask students to use the target language at all times, however unnatural or frustrating this may seem at first. Explain that a lot of the material has been specifically designed to teach and revise the key grammar points and if you talk in your mother tongue, this defeats the whole object of the exercise.

d Encourage a 'sharing mentality' by which students pool ideas and help each other. People learn better if they learn together.

e Vary the seating arrangements from day to day. This avoids having the same pairs or groups working together all the time.

f When doing group exercises, use the **north/east/west/south** format you see in a game of bridge. Such a structure allows people to talk to each other in comfort without having to shout or lean across at angles of 45 degrees.

g Introduce the concept of **cross setting** early on in the course and use it as often as you can. **Cross setting** is a very simple idea that can prove highly effective. You ask students to set exam style questions for other members of the class (as with the blank filling exercise on page 40) and then to mark the answers they get back from their class mates. This involves a considerable amount of time, thought and effort.

In order to set a question, the students need to think carefully about the language and structures they are using and try to 'get into the mind of the examiner.' Then, when marking the answers they get back, they have to be able to explain why one idea is right and another wrong.

h When doing the listening exercises, make sure that everyone understands the point and purpose of the exercise before you begin. While the tape is playing for the first time, write new vocabulary and grammar up on the board. Discuss this with the class before you play the tape again.

SECTION I 'The Italian Restaurant'

For the first two or three photograph exercises put the following diagram up on the board:

in the top left-hand corner	at the top	in the top right-hand corner
on the left	in the middle	on the right
in the bottom left-hand corner	at the bottom	in the bottom right-hand corner

Pre-teach expressions like:

in the foreground	just below	
in the background	in front of	
to the left of	behind	
to the right of	close to	
just above	next to	etc.

Use the photograph as the basis for a pair exercise with students 'interviewing' each other. Then expand this into a general class discussion, perhaps asking some of the following questions:

What is your favourite food?

Do you enjoy cooking? Why? Why not?

Are there any kinds of food you never eat?

Have you ever tried unusual or exotic food? (e.g. octopus, caviar etc.).

If so, can you describe the taste?

SECTION 2 'Paul's pie in the sky!'

• This article first appeared in the *News of the World* .

Use the text as the basis for a conversation between you and the class.

Ask students to define key words (*pizza, romantic, organise* etc.) and to identify any vocabulary or grammar points they don't understand.

Invite them to give their opinion about the story (e.g. Is it romantic or stupid to spend £5000 on eight pizzas?) and then ask supplementary questions prompted by the text. For example:

a What is the difference between *to remember* and *to remind* ?

b What else can you find in a pie? (e.g. meat, apple, mince)

and so on...

When the text is clear, set questions **A, B** and **C** as a classroom exercise to be done in pairs and then, after about fifteen minutes, go through the answers with the whole class.

A Vocabulary

1 recalled	6 limousine (limo)
2 dated	7 picked up
3 problem	8 delivered to
4 round the corner from	9 famous
5 old	10 hiring

B Comprehension

1 false	6 false
2 false	7 false
3 true	8 true
4 true	9 true
5 true	10 false

C Phrasal Verbs

When explaining a new phrasal verb, always give as many model sentences as you can. With number **3,** for example, you might say that *pick up* = 'collect', as in:

I'll *pick up* the dry cleaning on my way home.
The play starts at eight so I'll *pick you up* at seven-thirty.
Pick up the litter and put it in the bin.

Although this process is time-consuming, it does make the meaning absolutely clear.

D Summary

Set the summary for homework.

As mentioned in the Introductory Notes, **summary writing** is an ideal way of preparing students for the extended writing exercises of Papers 2 and 3.

Many students – even those who speak fluently – can feel uncomfortable about writing, so don't expect too much too soon. Build the foundations slowly and carefully, using summary writing as the 'brickwork'.

A summary is a short, structured, achievable task which can boost confidence and act as a vital bridge between making a sentence and creating a 180 word free-form essay.

For the student, it helps to establish vocabulary and grammar, and it develops a feel for the structure and flow of a foreign language. For the teacher, it gives a clear idea of how well the primary source material is being absorbed, offering insight into the individual strengths and weaknesses of each member of the class.

Summary writing is a much under-rated and much under-used tool. Set this type of exercise as often as you can.

SECTION 3 Boeing advert

Follow the same pattern that you used for the £5000 pizzas.

a Discuss the text.

b Develop the theme with a series of follow-up questions.

c Set the exercises as pair work.

d Check the answers with the whole class.

When discussing the text, you might like to ask:

What is the difference between 'a thousand people' and 'thousands of people'?
What else can 'ebb and flow'?
What do the phrasal verbs mean? *(taking off, goes on, adds up to)*

Follow-up questions:

Do you enjoy flying? Why? Why not?
Have you ever had a bad flight? If so, can you describe what happened?
Is the experience of flying any different from that of travelling by coach, ship or train?

B Vocabulary

1 jetliner	5 major
2 passengers	6 nearly
3 goes on	7 flying
4 around the clock	8 just

C Comprehension

1 false;   2 true;   3 true;   4 false;   5 true.

SECTION 4 Ladybird

You form **ladybird words** and **ladybird expressions** by putting together two or more simple nouns. Eg. *hot dog, butterfly, air traffic control tower, clothes horse, the day before yesterday* etc.

There are thousands of these simple compound noun forms in English and most people find them practical, relevant and easy to learn.

But you may like to point out that some **ladybirds** have unexpected meanings: you can't eat 'traffic jam'; a 'pigtail' is not the tail of a pig; and a 'ladybird' is neither a lady nor a bird.

There are six **ladybird** exercises in *Passport* and eight in *Personal Passport*.

SECTION 5 Pronunciation

Should you teach pronunciation at First Certificate level?

My personal view is that if students have wide-ranging exposure to the target language through TV, films, radio, records etc, there is little or no need for a formal teaching of pronunciation. For most people, the ear simply adjusts automatically and instinctively to the sounds it hears. Indeed, an over-emphasis on the subtleties of pronunciation can be both counterproductive and inhibiting.

However, if the class have little or no exposure to the target language and are conscious of particular difficulties like *b* and *p, th,* or *l* and *r,* you may need to ignore the above advice and focus on particular problem areas.

The exercise on page 12 is designed to 'test the water', helping you to understand how much guidance and practice the class might need. Questions **1** and **3** act as a kind of springboard for a general discussion about the subject. If lots of separate problems are raised, then you may need to go through them one by one over the next few weeks.

But only you can judge what the class really needs here. I don't think any general course book can deal with the welter of unknown variables and local factors that might apply.

- There are additional pronunciation exercises on pages 43 and 159.

SECTION 6 The definite article *the*

Perhaps start by asking the class if they can explain the various rules about the definite article.

> When do we use *the?*

> When don't we use *the?*

> What is the difference between the definite article *(the)* and the indefinite articles *(a* and *an)*?

Introduce and explain the listening exercise on page 13. Play the tape twice and then go through the answers to questions **1** and **4.**

For **Part B**, divide the class into pairs and play the tape for a third time. Check the answers for questions **5** to **12** and then go through the two columns (**A** and **B**) on page 14.

Ask why there are no definite articles in **Column A**.

It may take several minutes and various suggestions from you before the class come up with the answer that in **Column B** you are visiting these places, whereas in **Column A** you are using them for their primary purpose, e.g. to sue, to study, to pray, to get better etc.

Part A

1 true
2 true
3 *a*   true   *e*   false
   b   false   *f*   false
   c   false   *g*   true
   d   false   *h*   true

i	true	*l*	false
j	true	*m*	false
k	true	*n*	true

4 true

Part B

5 the piano, the flute, the guitar

6 breakfast, lunch, dinner

7 football, cricket, golf, tennis

8 Asia, Africa, Australasia

9 Everest, Kilimanjaro, Mount Fuji

10 the Andes, the Alps, the Himalayas

11 the Pacific, the Atlantic, the Indian Ocean

12 The more I eat, the fatter I get.

Interviewer:	On today's 'English by Radio', we're going to talk about the use of the definite article. I'm joined by Jane Pitman, Principal Lecturer in linguistics at the University of Leeds. Jane, it seems to me that the definite article is one of the most complicated parts of English grammar. Why is it so difficult?
Jane Pitman:	I think the reason is that although there are some basic rules about how and when to use *the*, there are also quite a lot of exceptions and these exceptions are not always very logical or easy to explain. It really needs a bit of patience, and it's not something you can learn overnight.
Interviewer:	You say there are some basic rules. Let's start with those.
Jane Pitman:	Well, you use the definite article in front of a single countable noun. You say, 'the house', 'the hat', 'the bird', and so on. And you also need it when you use a noun in a specific sense, as in a sentence like, 'I read the book she gave me.' – We're talking about a particular book here...
Interviewer:	So, we use it with single countable nouns and nouns used in a specific sense. Right, I think that's clear so far. But I suspect it gets a bit more difficult now.
Jane Pitman:	Well, it does, unfortunately. There are certain categories of noun – like the names of musical instruments or the names of different sports – that have their own rules. In other words, you have to know which category something belongs to before you can work out whether it needs a definite article or not. Now, in case that all sounds a bit confusing, let's go through some of the categories and see which ones need an article.
Interviewer:	OK. Let's start with musical instruments. What's the rule with that?
Jane Pitman:	Well, with musical instruments you always need a definite article. You say, 'I'm learning the piano,' 'She plays the flute,' 'My favourite instrument is the guitar,' and so on.

Interviewer:	OK. What about meals then?
Jane Pitman:	With those, there's no article. You say, 'What time do you have breakfast?' or, 'We had lunch an hour ago' or, 'Dinner is served at eight o'clock'.
Interviewer:	So the names of musical instruments need a definite article but the names of meals don't. I can't see the logic there.
Jane Pitman:	Well, that's exactly the point I was making earlier. I don't think there is any logic. It's just a matter of convention, style or habit.
Interviewer:	Right. Now, what about the names of sports?
Jane Pitman:	You never use an article with those. For instance, you say, 'They play football every Saturday', 'I love cricket', 'I prefer golf to tennis, etc.
Interviewer:	Now, let's come on to proper nouns – names spelt with a capital letter. What about countries and continents?
Jane Pitman:	You say, 'The dress was made an Italy', 'She comes from Japan', 'Have you ever been to Kenya?' So there's no article with the name of a country. And the same is true with the names of continents. You talk about Asia, Africa, Australasia and so on.
Interviewer:	What about mountains?
Jane Pitman:	Now, you have to be a bit careful here. It depends on whether you are referring to one mountain or a range of mountains. For Everest, Kilimanjaro, Mount Fuji and other individual mountains, there's no article. But when you talk about a range of mountains – like the Andes, the Alps or the Himalayas – then you must use the definite article.
Interviewer:	OK. So what about deserts and oceans?
Jane Pitman:	Oh, that's very straightforward. There's always an article. The Sahara, the Gobi, the Kalahari, or the Pacific, the Atlantic, the Indian Ocean, and so on.
Interviewer:	Right. Do seas, rivers and lakes need one too?
Jane Pitman:	Seas, yes. The Baltic Sea, the Caspian sea, the Irish Sea... Rivers, yes. The Thames, the Nile, the Orinoco... But lakes don't. Lake Geneva, Lake Constance, Lake Superior...
Interviewer:	There's one more category: islands.
Jane Pitman:	Well, with the name of a particular island you don't use an article. Malta, Sardinia, Cuba... But when you talk about a group of islands, well that's different, because then you do use an article. The Channel Islands, the Canaries, the West Indies etc.
Interviewer:	In fact, that's the same rule that we had for mountains.
Jane Pitman:	Yes, that's right. An individual mountain or an individual island has no article, a range of mountains or a group of islands does.
Interviewer:	Now, just changing the subject for a moment, what about a double comparative?
Jane Pitman:	Ah, this is a sentence or statement with two comparatives. Well, let me give you an example: 'The more I eat the fatter I get.' As you can see, there are definite articles in front of both of the comparatives.

Interviewer: Now, Jane, you've given us quite a lot of detailed information there... What's the best way to learn something as complicated at this?

Jane Pitman: I suppose my advice would be, take your time. Don't rush, and, above all, remember that a language is a strange creature. It's not a rational, mechanistic thing. You're not dealing with a computer. You can't complain when the grammar doesn't make sense – as is the case with the definite article. I think you just have to accept a language on its own terms, however moody and odd it may be...

You might like to set Sections 7, 8 and 10 for homework. Section 9, however, is probably best done in class.

SECTION 7 Prepositions of time

1 at . . . on	**9** on
2 on	**10** at
3 in	**11** at . . . on
4 in . . . in	**12** in
5 at	**13** in
6 in	**14** at
7 in	**15** in
8 at . . . in	

SECTION 8 Plurals

1 houses	**11** pins
2 mouse	**12** people
3 feet	**13** calf
4 peaches	**14** radios
5 men	**15** tooth
6 woman	**16** dishes
7 lives	**17** crises
8 knife	**18** apology
9 sheep	**19** countries
10 ponies	**20** trays

SECTION 9 Question words + *ever*

Write a summarised version of the information on pages 16 and 17 up on the board.

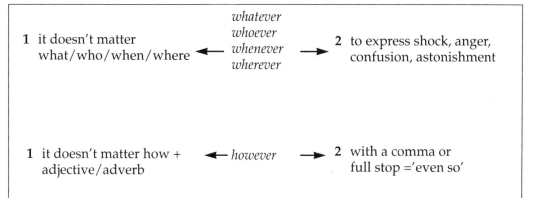

whyever expresses anger

Ask students to do the exercise at the bottom of page 17 in pairs.
Then check the answers with the whole class.

1 wherever	**6** whatever
2 whenever	**7** however
3 whatever	**8** however
4 whoever	**9** whenever
5 whyever	**10** wherever

SECTION 10 *make* and *do*

1 makes/made	**8** did
2 made	**9** makes/made/will make
3 do	**10** do/make
4 make	**11** does/did etc... makes/made etc.
5 make	**12** makes/made etc... does/did etc.
6 make	**13** making
7 do	**14** do

SECTION 11 Phrasal verb story

Use a consideration of the ten points on page 18 as a springboard for a general class discussion about the trials and tribulations of learning phrasal verbs. Ask some of the following questions:

What particular difficulties do you have with phrasal verbs?

Do you use them in your spoken English or do you try to avoid them whenever possible?

Does anyone have a 'method' for learning these verbs?

Do you have phrasal verbs in your mother tongue?

If so, do the equivalent verb and preposition combinations have the same meaning in the two languages?

Then, having considered the various points raised in the discussion, try to establish some method and pattern for that particular class, using the Angus Macpherson cartoon as a base.

SECTION 12 Phrasal verb story

The cartoon story that begins on page 19 contains some 325 phrasal and prepositional verbs and is a major feature of the book. You can use the material in a variety of ways, as I explain below, and some general advice about the process of learning phrasal verbs is given in the Study Skills section in Section 11.

However, before considering the function of the story, I'd like to make one important point about terminology. For the sake of clarity, I have made no distinction in the Student's Book between a 'phrasal verb' and a 'prepositional verb'. Nor have I tried to explain which of these verbs are 'transitive', 'intransitive', 'separable' or 'inseparable'. My experience is that such explanations serve only to confuse the student and will beg more questions than they answer. I think most people learn such verb forms by instinct rather than by logic. However, I accept that many teachers will disagree with this and will want to make such distinctions at the beginning of the course, perhaps as part of a general discussion on why these verb forms are so difficult to learn.

How to use the story:

Experiment with different techniques until you find one that suits your particular class. You might like to:

a go through the text explaining the phrasal verbs one by one;

b set the cartoon as a reading exercise for homework – then ask the follow-up questions in the Teacher's Book in the next lesson;

c ask students to write a 120 word summary of each chapter of the story;

d encourage the class to act out the story in the role-play exercise described on page 28.

Follow-up questions:

1 Why couldn't Angus get off to sleep?
2 What did he do with the belt?
3 What happened when Frederick caught sight of the belt with the keys?

SECTION 1 'The Gesture'

Follow the same pattern as in Unit 1, with pair work (describing a photograph) leading on to class discussion ('Gestures').

SECTION 2 Vocabulary Multiple Choice

Before setting Section 2 as a pair exercise, you might like to introduce and define the term **multiple choice**, explaining that this style of question ('choose the best answer *a*, *b*, *c*, or *d*') is found in Papers 1 and 4 of the exam.

1	*c*	edge	11 *a*	lose
2	*d*	nearly	12 *b*	loose
3	*b*	besides	13 *c*	check in
4	*a*	beside	14 *a*	check-out
5	*c*	hard	15 *b*	check up
6	*d*	hardly	16 *d*	cheque
7	*b*	heard	17 *b*	at least
8	*a*	herd	18 *c*	the latest
9	*c*	missed	19 *d*	the least
10	*d*	mist	20 *a*	at last

As you go through the answers, make some of the following points:

- Most adverbs end in *-LY* (e.g. quickly, slowly, easily), but you cannot say, 'He works hardly.'
  (Compare *hard* in question **5** with *hardly* in questions **6** and **16**.)
- *Lose* is the opposite of 'win'.
  Loose is the opposite of 'tight'.
- *stingy* = 'mean', tight-fisted'

Note the use of the **Past Perfect Continuous** in question **20** and perhaps consider the explanation of this tense in the Grammar Reference Section at the back of the book.

SECTION 3 'What do Puerto Ricans do...?'

- This article first appeared in the *Daily Mirror*.

As with the article on the £5000 pizzas and with the Boeing advert,

Unit 2

21

a Discuss the text.
b Develop the theme with a series of follow-up questions.
c Set exercises **A**, **B** and **C** as pair work.
d Check the answers with the whole class.

a When discussing the text, ask the class to explain the difference between...

- 'to spend time' and 'to waste time'

- 'to hold', 'to hug' and 'to cuddle'

- an acquaintance and a friend

...and point out that...

- the suffix *-ESS* often indicates a female noun (e.g. waitress, princess, actress, lioness, hostess)

- a *counsellor* advises whereas a *councillor* governs

- *research* is uncountable (e.g. 'Research has also revealed...')

- *whose* is normally followed by either a noun or the verb t*o be*.

b When developing the theme, cover some of the points in exercises **D** and **E**.

d When checking the material, write all the correct answers up on the board.

A Vocabulary

1	touchy	7	discarded
2	top	8	irritates
3	carried out	9	occur
4	just	10	significant
5	found	11	stiffen
6	though	12	tighten

B Comprehension

1 true; 2 false; 3 false; 4 true; 5 true; 6 false; 7 false; 8 true; 9 true; 10 true.

SECTION 4 Writing letters

Listening 1

George Davies: This is 'English by Radio', I'm George Davies, and on today's programme we're going to look at the structure of a letter... And I'm joined once more this morning by Jane Pitman...

Jane Pitman: Good morning, George... Good morning, everyone...

George Davies: ...who we seem to be keeping very busy at the moment! Now, Jane, we get quite a lot of correspondence from listeners on this particular subject, so could you give us some general advice about the best way to lay out a letter? For example, are there any fixed rules for doing it?

Jane Pitman: Well. I wouldn't say there are absolutely fixed rules, but, as with many things, there are conventions, styles, traditions, that most people follow.... And I think there are probably eight basic points to bear in mind.

George Davies:	OK. Perhaps we could go through them one by one?
Jane Pitman:	Well, let's start at the top of the page and work down... The first point I'd make is that you should put your address and postcode in the top right–hand corner of the page.
George Davies:	Aha.
Jane Pitman;	The second point is, put your telephone number directly below the post code.
George Davies:	OK.
Jane Pitman:	Then thirdly, put the date directly below the telephone number.
George Davies:	So all those things are on the right-hand side of the page: address, post code, telephone number, and date.
Jane Pitman:	Yes, that's right. Now the fourth point is that on the next line down – but this time on the left-hand side of the page – you put what's called the 'salutation' or greeting. 'Dear Fred', 'Dear Mrs Thompson', 'Dear Sir or Madam' etc. And this is always followed by a comma.
George Davies:	Not an exclamation mark.
Jane Pitman:	No, it must be a comma. Then we come on to the structure of the main text. So, my fifth point would be that the opening paragraph should be quite short. You can use the opening paragraph to introduce yourself, to say who you are, or to thank the other person for their letter... or to explain why you are writing. But, as I say, this part of the letter should never be more than a few lines long.
George Davies:	OK.
Jane Pitman:	Now, sixth: the second and third paragraphs are usually longer than the first. They contain the main details of the letter – what some people call 'the meat in the sandwich'.
George Davies:	Right.
Jane Pitman:	Then, the seventh point is that, in the final, short paragraph, you give instructions or make a request. You explain what you would like the other person to do. You know, something along the lines of, 'I would be grateful if you could send me the cheque immediately' or 'Please give my best wishes to Fred', or 'Write soon!' or whatever... And then finally – and this is again on the left-hand side – you sign off with an expression like 'Yours faithfully' (for a formal letter to someone you don't know) or 'Yours sincerely' (if you've written the surname of the person in the salutation) or 'with best wishes', 'with love', 'with all my love' etc. (if it's someone you're close to), followed by your signature...
	(fade)

Listening 2

1 Dear Sir,

   Three weeks ago I bought a woollen jumper at your store...

   I would be most grateful if you could send me a full refund as soon as possible.

   Yours faithfully,

   Emma Jones

2 Dear Ken,

I've got a problem and I need your advice...

And so what do you think I should do? Please write soon.

Love,

Sue

3 Dear Sir or Madam,

I am writing in response to your advertisement in today's newspaper for a junior accounts clerk to work in your international loans department...

I have enclosed my CV and would be happy to come in for an interview at any time that is convenient for you.

Yours faithfully,

Nina Bradd

4 Dear Mrs Lewis,

On my return home from work yesterday, I found your dog 'Benjy' pulling up the rhubarb in my back garden...

Please understand that should you or your dog enter my garden again without my express permission, I shall have no alternative but to take appropriate legal action to protect my property against trespassers.

Yours sincerely,

David Davidson

5 Dear Frank,

Thanks for your letter! It was great to hear from you again! I'm sorry I didn't write before but I've been up to my eyes in work!...

That's all for now! Give my love to Sally and the kids. Hope to see you soon.

Love,

Karen

SECTION 5 Ladybird

This list of questions can be used in two ways.

1 At the beginning of the lesson, divide the class into pairs and ask everyone to interview their partner, asking him or her these twenty questions. Emphasise that the exercise should be done without notes.

Some time later (at the end of the class perhaps), put the pairs back together and see how much people can remember about their partners. The conversation might begin: 'You told me that you are left-handed, that you don't think horseshoes bring good luck, that you can keep a secret, and that you never bite your nails...'

Alternatively:

2 Divide the class into large groups of about six or seven, and explain that the twenty questions are a **Compatibility Test**. By comparing your answers with someone else's, you can discover how compatible the two of you are.

Then write the following table up on the board:

less than 10 answers in common	**not compatible at all**
10 to 12	**fairly compatible**
13 to 16	**very compatible**
17 to 20	**unbelievable!**

Explain that the idea here is to use the twenty questions to find out which member of your group is most compatible with you.

Once you have set up the exercise, just 'disappear'. Don't suggest how the interviewing should be done. Let the groups work this out for themselves. And don't go round the class, as you might do with other group exercises. In this game, the less the students see of you the better.

After some initial hesitation, the groups will probably adopt one of two methods:

Either *a* everyone will interview everyone else 'one to one'
or *b* a 'chairman' will read out the questions and then go round the group noting down answers in a grid.

As you may have noticed, most of the questions are clear-cut, requiring simple 'yes' or 'no' answers, but a few of them – **14, 15** and **19**, for example – are intentionally vague. This deliberate vagueness will trigger off further discussion within the group similar to that generated by certain comparisons in the Order of Size exercise on page 124.

When the groups have finished, ask individual members of the class who they were most compatible with.

- Did any pair score 18 or more?

- Were there any surprising answers?

SECTION 6 Dishwash electric advert

A Vocabulary

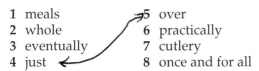

1 meals   5 over
2 whole   6 practically
3 eventually   7 cutlery
4 just   8 once and for all

B Interpretation

6 *practically*   =   'almost'
8 *cutlery*   =   knives, forks, spoons.
   crockery   =   cups, plates, saucers, etc.

Follow-up discussion:

Ask how many people in the class have to wash up every day.
    How do they feel about this?
    Does anyone enjoy housework?

Bring similar short adverts into the class and use them as the basis for a **cross-setting** exercise (see page 11 of the Introductory Notes) based on the format below:

a vocabulary questions
b comprehension questions
c explanation of the phrasal verbs
d follow-up discussion.

SECTION 7 *so/such/such a/such an*

Board Summary

As you go through the explanation on page 28, you may like to summarise this information on the board, along the lines of:

so	+	adjective adverb
such a *such an*	+	adjective + singular noun
such	+	adjective + plural noun.

The **board summary** has three particular advantages:

a It clarifies the key points.
b It acts as an additional point of reference while students are doing the exercises.
c You can point to the relevant section of the board when explaining the answers.

Exercise 1

1 so
2 such a
3 so
4 such
5 so
6 such an
7 so
8 so
9 such a
10 so
11 such an
12 such an

Exercise 2

1 It was so cold that the river froze.
2 These shoes are so comfortable that I wear them all the time.
3 She was so hungry that she ate twenty-three packets of crisps.
4 It's such an old car that it belongs in a museum.
5 It was such a wonderful holiday that I didn't want to come home.
6 We were so late that we missed the train.
7 It's such a beautiful film that I've seen it eleven times.
8 I was so tired that I fell asleep on the bus.
9 The fog was so thick that they closed the airport.
10 He was so nervous that his hands were shaking.

SECTION 8 The emphatic use of *too*

Exercise 3

1	too many	**6**	too much
2	too much	**7**	too much
3	much too	**8**	much too
4	too many	**9**	much too
5	much too	**10**	too much

• *Information*, *air* and *violence* are uncountable.

SECTION 9 *some/any*

As with Section 6, write a summary on the board:

SOME	ANY
+ positive verb	+ negative verb
• for offers and requests	• most questions

SECTION 10 Ladybird

SECTION 11 *get*

Before playing the tape, go through the table on page 31 and consider these eight different meanings in some detail. Give additional examples as and when necessary.

Also, make the point that these meanings often overlap. For example, there are times when *receive* = 'earn', *collect* = 'fetch' and *arrive* = 'move'. So more than one answer may be correct.

Emphasise the opening sentence ('Perhaps *get* is the most difficult, flexible and useful word in English') and explain that this is not a grammar point that you can learn overnight. As with the definite article, it takes some time, but it's time well spent.

1 I'm getting tired. *(become)*
2 She gets £10 an hour. *(earn)*
3 We got back at 6.45. *(arrive)*
4 She got 92% in her maths exam. *(earn)*
5 Where did you get that painting? *(buy)*
6 Get your feet off the sofa! *(move)*
7 Where can I get Italian newspapers? *(buy)*
8 I got a letter from my cousin yesterday. *(receive)*
9 Get me the manager! *(fetch)*
10 I'm getting really fed up with my job! *(become)*

11 What time did you get to Paris? *(arrive)*
12 Did you get my letter? *(receive)*
13 It's me. I'm at the station. Can you come and get me? *(collect)*
14 I got really angry. *(become)*
15 Get out! *(move)*

SECTION 12 Differences

SECTION 13 Phrasal verb story

Role Play

Not all classes enjoy role play exercises, but acting out the Angus Macpherson story on a regular basis can be an effective visual way of learning phrasal verbs.

You'll need a narrator to put the dialogue into context ('Sir Gerald Prescott was sitting at his desk reading *The Times*' etc.) and actors to play the leading roles:

a Sir Gerald Prescott
b Lady Prescott
c Angus Macpherson
d Karen Blackstone
e Lady Prescott's mother
f Lady Prescott's father
g Frederick Carruthers
h Mrs Carruthers
i Karen Blackstone's secretary
j Mr Thomas, the prison guard
k the night guard at Newtown jail

Those not wanting to act may like to take responsibility for sound effects (trains pulling into stations, cars roaring down motorways, a flat tyre hissing like a snake etc.) or props (a bunch of keys, a yellow diary, the tea bag used for a week etc).

Follow-up questions:

1 What suddenly dawned on Angus?
2 Where was Sir Gerald sitting?
3 Why did he tear up his *Times* and burst into tears?

SECTION 1 'The Girls' School'

Follow the pattern you have established in the first two units:

a   pair work (considering questions **1** to **6** together)

b   a general class discussion of the theme (questions **7** and **8**).

SECTION 2 Vocabulary multiple choice

1	*d*	a	**11**	*c*	seat
2	*b*	to	**12**	*b*	all
3	*c*	work	**13**	*b*	passengers
4	*a*	by	**14**	*d*	reading
5	*a*	commuter	**15**	*b*	ignoring
6	*d*	follow	**16**	*a*	arrive
7	*b*	get	**17**	*b*	tram
8	*a*	season	**18**	*c*	reach
9	*c*	catch	**19**	*b*	make
10	*c*	platform	**20**	*d*	too

Set this as a pair exercise and then go through the answers with the whole class.

For questions **5, 10, 11, 13, 14** and **17**, explain or elicit the key differences between the four words given.

For questions **7, 16,** and **18,** explain that:

   get to = arrive at = reach = come to

Point out that although these forms share a common meaning, *get, arrive* and *come* are used with different prepositions and *reach* is used without a preposition.

SECTION 3 'Balloony Branson's UFO prank backfires'

• This article first appeared in the *Sun*.

You won't find *balloony* in the dictionary. It's a word invented by the *Sun* to describe someone who does 'mad' ('loony') things in a balloon.

This is a typical **tabloid** article, with puns, slang and invented words woven into a dramatic 'human interest' story.

At some time in the course, you may like to compare the **popular press** (the *Sun*, the *Daily Mirror*, the *Star*, *Today*, the *Daily Mail*, the *Daily Express*, the *News of the World*, the *People*, the *Evening Standard* etc.) with the **quality press** (the *Daily Telegraph*, *The Times*, the *Guardian*, the *Independent*, the *Observer*, the *Financial Times* etc).

What are the differences between these two groups?
What are the similarities?
What about the style, content and design of each paper?
What political opinions or social attitudes do they represent?
Who buys them?
Why do people buy one paper rather than another?

Unit 3

If you have the resources available, take copies of different English language newspapers into the classroom and ask students to consider the various questions above. This could lead on to a more open-ended discussion:

What papers do members of the class read?
What do you buy a paper for? Information? Entertainment? Gossip?

Ask one or two members of the class to prepare a short speech for the next lesson outlining what their national press is like.

When going through the 'Balloony Branson' text, you might like to make the following points:

- *See* often means 'understand', as in 'I see', 'I see what you mean', or, 'Police and local residents did not see the joke.'
- *Evidence* is uncountable (e.g. 'If there is sufficient evidence...')

As far as grammar is concerned, explain how we often use verbs like *say, believe, think, know* and *understand* in a particular way. For example:

'....where the little green men *were believed* to have touched down....'
'She *is said* to be the richest woman in the world'.
'The robbers *are thought* to have escaped through a side door.'

Exercise B

1	massive	6	aliens
2	terrified	7	touched down
3	glowing	8	tripped
4	crept	9	sufficient
5	realised	10	unrepentant

C Comprehension

1 true; 2 false; 3 false; 4 true; 5 false; 6 true; 7 false; 8 false; 9 false; 10 false.

D Explanations

1 They were afraid (?) ...shocked (?) ...trying to escape (?).
2 To avoid the balloon which was drifting towards the airport.
3 In a field near Redhill in Surrey.
4 truncheons
5 5 am
6 Kenley, South London
7 There were accidents, people were afraid etc.
8 She ran out in a panic, tripped and nearly broke her neck.

SECTION 4 Voyager 2

This is the first exam style listening exercise in the book and it may be an opportune moment to explain how Paper 4 works.

There will normally be three different types of listening exercise. The **gap-filling** and **true/false** exercises test the ability to listen for specific information, while the **multiple choice** tests for general meaning.

Each passage is played twice.

Interviewer: Since its launch in 1977, the American spaceprobe Voyager 2 has travelled five billion kilometres through space and sent back pictures of Saturn, Uranus, Jupiter and Neptune that have transformed our view of the solar system. On tonight's edition of 'Science World', I'm joined by Dr Alison Rawsthorn, one of the advisers on the Voyager 2 project. Alison, perhaps I could begin by asking you to explain the background to this extraordinary adventure.

Dr Alison Rawsthorn: Yes, well, every 176 years, Saturn, Uranus, Jupiter and Neptune move into what is roughly a straight line. We realised that if we could calculate the launch date accurately, we would be able to visit four different planets with a single probe and then use the gravitational field of Neptune to push the machine out of our solar system and off into deep space. This was a once-in-a-lifetime opportunity and it was much too good to miss.

Interviewer: So, let's go through the mission stage by stage. When did it all begin?

Dr Alison Rawsthorn: Well, Voyager 2 was launched on 20th August 1977, and after some initial problems with the navigational equipment, it reached Jupiter on 9th July 1979. And that's when we made the first major discoveries of the trip. Over the next few hours, we identified three new moons, as well as volcanoes and dust rings that nobody had ever seen before. Then it was on to the next planet, Saturn, which we got to on August 25th 1981. Now, everybody knows that Saturn has rings, but until Voyager, we didn't realise that these rings were made up of thousands of bands of light, each 35 metres wide. I remember the day when the first pictures came back showing us these bands in close-up. There was tremendous excitement in the control centre – it seemed as if every photograph was teaching us something new about space. And then a few days later, Voyager began the five-year journey on to Uranus.
Now at this point, there was a long and passionate political debate in America. Many people wanted to abandon the mission. They thought it was a waste of money. But eventually it was decided to carry on, and by the time we got to the strange magnetic fields of Uranus on 24th January 1986 and the 'ice planet' Neptune on August 24th 1989, I think there was genuine public support for what we were doing.

Interviewer: Now, the last planet of the four, Neptune, has always seemed something of a mystery to me. Just how much do we know about it?

Dr Alison Rawsthorn: Well, in fact Galileo spotted Neptune in 1613, but he didn't realise it was a planet. He thought it was just a moon going round Jupiter, and it wasn't until the nineteenth century, in 1846, that we identified it properly. It's not a very inviting place. The atmosphere contains methane and hydrogen but there's no oxygen there. It's cold and stormy with winds of up to 640 kilometres an hour and there are these extraordinary ice volcanoes that are a complete puzzle. We just have no idea what they are.

Interviewer: So at this stage, Voyager was twelve years into its journey.

Dr Alison Rawsthorn: Yes, and we were beginning to have problems communicating with the probe. You see, Neptune is 4.1 billion kilometres from the earth and, at that distance, a signal from Voyager travelling at the speed of light takes 4 hours and 6 minutes to reach our tracking stations in America, Spain, Japan and Australia. As you can imagine, the signal gets very weak after all that time. And there's also another difficulty when dealing with such distances. Voyager is travelling at 16 kms per second and so by the time the signals get back to earth, the spacecraft has moved on another 250,000 kilometres. This means that before we can send new instructions to the probe, we have to do some calculations to work out where it is! It's not like dealing with a fixed object. It all gets very complicated!

Interviewer: Alison, you told us that Voyager has now left our solar system and is travelling on into deep, interstellar space. Now this may seem a strange question, but what would happen if at some point in the future someone or something from another world came into contact with the spaceprobe? Would they know what it was? Or would they think it was just a piece of junk floating around in space?

Dr Alison Rawsthorn: Well, that's a fascinating question. Are we alone in the universe or is there life on other planets? We have telescopes and computers and antennae down here on earth but we don't really know who or what is out there deep in space in other galaxies. So just in case Voyager does have a 'close encounter of the third kind', we decided to fill the spaceprobe with information about our planet. For example, on one of the front panels we've put a drawing of a man and a woman and a map of our solar system with a sign pointing to the earth. And then if you open up the main door, you can find 155 photographs to show what our world looks like. For example, there are pictures of the Sydney Opera House, the Taj Mahal, the Great Wall of China, some of the colleges at Oxford University and so on.

There's also a copper-plated disc inside called 'The Sounds of Earth' and, when you play the disc, using the special needle provided, you can hear greetings in sixty different languages, a mother singing a lullaby, the sound of a kiss, rain, surf, a volcano erupting, a tractor, footsteps, heartbeats, laughter, a baby crying and the calling of a whale. There's also four kinds of music – rock, jazz, folk and classical – and a special message from Jimmy Carter, who was the American President when Voyager was launched. Now the idea is that if an intelligent life form came into contact with the probe, they would have enough information to be able to work out what human beings look like, what sort of creatures we are, where we live, how we live, and so on. And perhaps this would encourage 'them' to come and make contact with 'us.' Who knows? Maybe at this very moment, an alien from outer space is listening to our recordings of Mozart and Beethoven, looking at a picture of the Great Wall of China, and planning a quick tourist visit to planet earth. It's a nice idea. But until that happens, Voyager is just continuing on, deeper and deeper into space, ready for its next major 'appointment', a meeting with the dog star Sirius in 300,000 years' time...

SECTION 5 Question tags

1 You're a doctor, *aren't you?*
2 They haven't arrived yet, *have they?*
3 It's hot today, *isn't it?*
4 He's a good teacher, *isn't he?*
5 She speaks English, *doesn't she?*
6 They're not taking the exam, *are they?*
7 Rangoon is in Burma, *isn't it?*
8 They went to Canada last year, *didn't they?*
9 He doesn't eat meat, *does he?*
10 She looks very happy, *doesn't she?*
11 You didn't tell him the secret, *did you?*
12 She's working very hard, *isn't she?*
13 You can't come on Monday, *can you?*
14 You can come on Monday, *can't you?*
15 He needs a holiday, *doesn't he?*

SECTION 6

Since there is so much information here, write a board summary of pages 41 and 42, along the lines of:

PRESENT SIMPLE	PRESENT CONTINUOUS
every day	temporary
regular	future
you can predict it	
adds -s in 3rd person singular	*am / is / are + -ING*

Then set the exercise on page 42.

SECTION 7

This '11 to 16' exercise starts off as pair work and then leads on to an extended writing exercise.

The 200 word essay could be set for homework, but it actually works much better if the writing is done in class, straight after the two interviews have been completed.

SECTION 8 Homophones

Go through the rubric for **Exercise 1** and explain that the class are going to hear twenty common words which they should write down in the appropriate spaces. Then divide the class into pairs. Play the tape once without interruption and then ask what the last eighteen words have in common.

Go through the explanation of **homophones** at the bottom of the page and then set question **5**: 'What are the two possible spellings for sounds **5** to **20**?'

When checking the answers, put both spellings up on the board and consider any pronunciation points raised (e.g. the difference between 'where' and 'were', or 'right' and 'ride').

For **Exercise 2**, ask the class to write down the whole sentence before deciding which of the two possible spellings (and meanings) of the **homophone** is being used. Use the pause button at the end of each sentence. Put the students back in their original pairs for **Exercise 3** and explain that the idea here is to make up new sentences that include one of the two **homophones** listed at the end of each line.

- The first of the pair reads their sentences to a partner.
- He or she writes them down and then decides which of the homophones is being used.
- He or she then reads the first student his or her fifteen sentences.
- The first student writes them down and decides which of the homophones is being used.

Exercise 1

1	tourist		11	where	*(wear)*
2	potato		12	so	*(sew)*
3	see	*(sea)*	13	deer	*(dear)*
4	bear	*(bare)*	14	none	*(nun)*
5	steel	*(steal)*	15	hour	*(our)*
6	weather	*(whether)*	16	tail	*(tale)*
7	piece	*(peace)*	17	night	*(knight)*
8	there	*(their)*	18	right	*(rite)*
9	here	*(hear)*	19	eight	*(ate)*
10	road	*(rode)*	20	sale	*(sail)*

Exercise 2

Example: She arrived at half past eight.
1 *There* was a great film on TV last night.
2 It was a *waste* of money.
3 My aunt has a very narrow *waist*.
4 The *road* was bumpy.
5 I was stung by a *bee*.
6 He must *be* very rich.
7 Can you *sew* this button on for me?
8 The lift is out of order. You'll have to use the *stairs*.
9 What was the *weather* like?
10 I don't know *whether* she'll come.
11 Who *ate* my porridge?
12 He got on the motorbike and *rode* off.

13 It's made of *steel*.
14 *Where* did you put my jacket?
15 She ate nine *pieces* of chocolate.
16 *Would* you pass me the salt, please?
17 My *aunt* has a very narrow waist.
18 Why *aren't* you coming to the party?
19 What did you say that *for*?
20 It took me an *hour* and a half to get here.

SECTION 9 The answerphone

Go through the rubric at the top of page 45 and then play the tape twice, perhaps following the general outline described in the Introductory Notes (page 11).

The Totally Truthful Travel Company reappears on page 58.

Answers:

1 17th May.
Scottish...Three...of...save.
5p
2 Tuesday...3.45.
256 2629
3 delighted
board...Thursday...11.00.
4 £154.87
9 – 5.30... 9 – 11.30
5 compact discs...in
6 keep-fit...143...second
7 081-602 3914
8 the police station.

Hello, Mrs Sullivan? This is the Manchester Public Lending Library. Erm, we're ringing about some books you borrowed. There were four altogether, and you should have returned them on May 17th. So, erm, they're a bit overdue now, and we thought we'd just give you a call to remind you, er, just in case you'd forgotten ... Now, according to our records, you have the following books out on loan at the moment. Let me just see. Oh, erm, yes. There's Famous Scottish Ghost Stories, erm, Learn Japanese in Three Weeks, erm, The Guinness Book of Records, and, er, finally, 101 ways to save money. Oh, and by the way, because these books are all overdue, you'll have to pay a fine, erm, on each one. And that's 5p per book per day... Thank you...

This is Mr Allen's nurse speaking. You rang us about an appointment with the dentist. We've had a cancellation for this Tuesday at 3.45. I hope that's OK. If you can't make it, perhaps you could call me here at the surgery. The number is 256 2629.

Carol, this is Debbie from the office. Welcome back. I hope you had a good holiday? I just rang to say that the Chairman was delighted with your report and he wants you to come to the next board meeting. That's on Thursday. It's at eleven o'clock in the conference room and it should take a couple of hours or so... Anyway, I'll see you in the office on Monday and I'll tell you all about it then...

Mrs Sullivan. This is the garage. We've fitted the new brake pads onto the car. But, erm, it took us a bit longer than we thought. Erm, as you know, we had estimated it would cost around £65 but, er, unfortunately, erm, I'm afraid we're going to have to revise that figure, erm, and the bill is going to be just a tiny bit higher than we expected... It's going to work out at, er, £154.87 – er, but that's inclusive of VAT and the good news is that we checked all the tyres and lights and everything and they're fine... The car is ready and you can come and pick it up any time you like... We're open from 9 to 5.30 during the week and from 9 to 11.30 on Saturday mornings.

This is the HMV record shop in Tanley Street. You ordered some compact discs. Erm, we had a delivery this morning and they're all in stock now, so, er, if you'd like to come in and get them, er, they'll be here...

Oh, Carol, it's Jo... Just thought I'd ring to tell you they've had a burst pipe at the fitness centre and the ground floor is flooded. You don't need gym shoes any more, you need wellington boots... Anyway, the keep fit class is now going to be in room 143 on the second floor. I'll see you there...

Carol... This is Alan Mitchell... Could you call me on 081-612 3914... Thanks.

Oh, erm... I was trying to contact the police station but I think I may have dialled the wrong number... Oh... erm... er...

SECTION 10 Phrasal verb story

Follow-up questions:

1 Why did Sir Gerald burst into tears?
2 How many prisoners had run away that week?
3 Who is going to run away to a run-down area?
4 What would happen if Lady Prescott ran away to a run-down area of Birmingham?
5 If she runs over Sir Gerald, what might she run into?

SECTION 1 'The Couple'

SECTION 2 Vocabulary multiple choice

Ask the students to do these twenty questions in pairs, and then go through the answers with the whole class.

1	*a*	for	11	*a*	whole
2	*c*	much	12	*c*	stirring
3	*d*	estate agent	13	*c*	overgrown
4	*c*	to buy	14	*c*	thing
5	*a*	understand	15	*d*	creak
6	*d*	running	16	*b*	warns
7	*c*	wrong	17	*c*	radiation
8	*c*	leaks	18	*c*	stop
9	*c*	happens	19	*a*	bargain
10	*d*	track	20	*a*	want

For question **1**, explain the difference between *for, since, during* and *while.*

   a *For* is followed by an expression that tells you **how long** something has been going on.
        eg.'We have been trying to sell our house *for* six months now.'
   b *Since* is followed by a word or expression that tells you **when** the activity began.
        eg.'We have been trying to sell our house *since* January.'
   c *During* is normally followed by a **noun.**
        eg.*during* the night.
   d *While* is normally followed by either a **gerund** or a **noun** plus a **verb.**
        eg.*While* eating, the monks never talk to each other.
        eg.*While* they are eating, the monks never talk to each other.

For question **3**, explain what the other agents do.

For question **10**, check the pronunciation (and meaning) of *trick, truck, trek* and *track.*

For question **16,** explain how *to alarm* means 'to frighten' and contrast the two adjectives *alarm* and *alarming.*

*   *alarm*   =   'warning,' as in 'alarm bell' and 'alarm clock'
*   *alarming* =   'frightening,' as in, 'There's been an *alarming* increase in serious crime over the past few years'.

SECTION 3 'The yuppie conmen trick home hunters'

*   This article first appeared in the *Evening Standard.*

Start by explaining the meaning of *con, conman* and *hoax.*

Once again, use the text as the basis for a conversation between you and the class. Ask for definitions of key words. Find out if there are any points of vocabulary or grammar that need to be explained. Ask for a reaction to the story eg.'Were Claire and Melanie unlucky or stupid? (**10,** exercise **C**). And so on...

Set exercises **B, C** and **D** as a pair exercise and then, fifteen minutes later, go through the answers with the whole class.

Unit 4

B Vocabulary

1	smart	6	punch
2	horrified	7	discussing
3	a minimum of	8	deal
4	actually	9	by mistake
5	delighted	10	concerned

C Comprehension

1 £850 (£425 each)
2 a housing association
3 14
4 in St Katharine's Dock
5 'Tim Hutton' – charming, 30, tanned, wearing an Armani suit
   'Dave Bishop' – 24, 6ft tall, well-dressed
6 They discovered that his 'home' number was that of a bank.
7 When she saw another man 'moving in'.
8 *'I smelled a rat '* = 'I knew that something was wrong'
9 These words are not being used in their literal sense.
10 *(for general discussion)*

SECTION 4 *Have*

Explain the three key meanings of *have*, giving additional examples if necessary.

Play the tape at least twice, pausing at the end of each sentence.

Write the answers up on the board, underlining:

a   the **past participle** that follows *has, have* or *had* in type 1 sentences;

b   the *to* + **infinitive** found in type 3 sentences.

1 Have you seen my watch anywhere? *(1 auxiliary)*
2 There are too many mistakes in this letter. You'll have to type it again. *(3 obligation)*
3 Can I have a glass of water? *(2 main verb)*
4 She has four brothers and five sisters. *(2 main verb)*
5 I have just got your message. *(1 auxiliary)*
6 They had to pay a fine of £250. *(3 obligation)*
7 You'll have to speak up. I can't hear you. *(3 obligation)*
8 We have considered your proposal very carefully. *(1 auxiliary)*
9 She has a very strange sense of humour. *(2 main verb)*
10 I start work at six... so I have to get up at about five. *(3 obligation)*
11 He has 89 pairs of shoes... *(2 main verb)*
12 ...and I have to clean them! *(3 obligation)*
13 We have lived here for twenty years. *(1 auxiliary)*
14 You shouldn't have told him! *(1 auxiliary)*
15 Shall we have a break? *(2 main verb)*

SECTION 5 Infinitive words and expressions

Go through the six terms introduced on page 52 and then ask the class to make up sentences featuring the infinitive words listed on page 53.

As the suggestions are made, write them up on the board, underlining first the **infinitive word** and then the **infinitive** that follows it.

Then go through the rubric of **Exercise 1** and ask the students to complete the ten questions in pairs.

When checking the answers once again, identify both the **infinitive word** and the **infinitive.** Although this may seem repetitive, bear in mind that many languages have no equivalent to **infinitive words, infinitive expressions, gerund word**s and **gerund expressions.**

Among the many possible answers for these exercises are:

Exercise 1

1	eat	6	go
2	buy	7	wear
3	drink	8	interrupt
4	rain	9	tell... believe
5	watch	10	hear

For question **2,** point out that *furniture* is always uncountable.

In question **4,** *get* = 'become.'

Exercise 2

1	go	4	pay
2	have	5	score
3	climb	6	go

For question **2,** connect *look, seem* and *sound,* and explain that these verbs are often followed by an **adjective** or an **adverb.**

> eg. 'You *look better* today.'
> 'She *seems happy.*'
> 'He *sounded* a bit *upset.*'

SECTION 6 *enough*

Go through the three model sentences at the bottom of page 54 and then ask students to give you a sentence for each of the nine examples at the top of page 55. Write the sentences up on the board.

Make an additional point about the use of *for* and *to* in sentences such as:

> 'I don't have enough time to deal with it now.'
> 'Is that jacket big enough for you?'

Explain how you often use... *'enough... to'* with a **verb**
and *'enough... for'* with a **noun.**

The advert at the bottom of page 55 is for Lloyds Bank.

SECTION 7 Choosing a suitable reply

Go through the rubric at the top of the page, explaining that the class are going to hear eighteen short sentences which they should write down in the appropriate spaces. They should then decide which of the three suggested answers would be the most appropriate.

Use the pause button as necessary at the end of each sentence.

While checking this exercise, ask the class for suitable questions for the other two answers.

• **cross-setting** (See Introductory Notes, page 11.)

1 How old is she?   Three and a half.
2 What's the time?
3 When did they arrive?
4 I've got toothache.
5 Where do you come from?
6 Would you like a cup of coffee?
7 Do you like coffee?
8 How do you like your coffee?
9 Which one do you want?
10 Have you worked out the answer?
11 Did you tell her the secret?
12 What was he writing?
13 What was he riding?
14 How did you get here?
15 I love jazz.
16 What did she do yesterday afternoon?
17 What did she do with her towel?
18 She told me she was the President of Venezuela.

Answers:

1 *b* three and a half
2 *c* half past three
3 *b* yesterday afternoon
4 *a* You should go and see a dentist.
5 *b* Madrid
6 *b* No thanks, I've just had one.
7 *a* Yes, I do.
8 *c* White with two sugars.
9 *c* the pink one
10 *c* Yes, I have.
11 *c* Yes, I did.
12 *b* A love letter
13 *a* A grey horse
14 *a* by bus
15 *a* So do I.
16 *a* She lay on the beach.
17 *b* She laid it on the beach.
18 *c* She was lying.

SECTION 8 Ladybird

	kitchen	bathroom	bedroom	sitting room
1 a work top	✓			
2 a dish cloth	✓			
3 toilet paper		✓		
4 a teaspoon	✓			
5 a hairdrier			✓	
6 a cooker	✓			
7 a soap dish		✓		
8 a bookcase				✓
9 a bedside lamp			✓	
10 a record player				✓
11 a clothes horse		✓		
12 a coffee table				✓
13 a toothbrush		✓		
14 a paper weight				✓
15 a washing machine	✓			
16 a dishwasher	✓			
17 a hot water bottle			✓	
18 a coat hanger			✓	
19 a bottle opener	✓			
20 an armchair				✓
21 an easy chair				✓
22 a pillow case			✓	

Certain of these items will have more than one answer.

SECTION 9 Differences

SECTION 10 Phrasal verb story

Follow-up questions:

1 What six things did Sir Gerald offer to do?
2 Why did Sir Gerald burst into tears?
3 What is the difference between 'walking out of a room' and 'storming out of a room'?
4 Who blows up all the time?
5 Who burst into tears?

SECTION 1 'The Market'

SECTION 2 Vocabulary multiple choice

This is a revision exercise. All these sentences have appeared before, but this time different words are missing.

1	c	speaks	11	b	leaves
2	b	to	12	b	compartments
3	a	plane	13	a	means
4	d	wisdom	14	c	get
5	d	off	15	d	tired
6	b	advise	16	a	to sell
7	d	hardly	17	a	reason
8	c	commute	18	d	weeds
9	c	always	19	d	shakes
10	d	barrier	20	b	real

SECTION 3 'Dolphins save surf boy...'

- This article first appeared in the *Sun*.

Perhaps start by asking the class to consider the language used in the text.

How does the writer 'dramatise' the story?
What effect do words like *grabbed*, *chunk* and *yelled* have?

Then ask them to write a similar dramatic or sensational story.

One way of doing this is to divide the class up into groups. Ask each group to write a 'boring' story.
eg. 'This morning I got up and went downstairs and had breakfast...'

They then exchange this for a 'boring' story from another group.

Each group now 'dramatises' or 'sensationalises' the 'boring' story they have received.
eg. 'At the crack of dawn, as a burning sun blazed through my window, I jumped out of bed and rushed down the stairs...' etc.

B Vocabulary

1	school	6	yelling
2	let him go	7	freaked out
3	head-butted... struck	8	gaping
4	chunk	9	in distress
5	came back	10	approximately

C Comprehension

1 false; 2 true; 3 false; 4 false; 5 true; 6 false; 7 false; 8 true; 9 false; 10 true.

- *School* is the group name for whales, porpoises, dolphins, etc.
  Shoal is used for a large group of small fish swimming together.

Unit 5

- 'a race' (the **noun**) can be *slow or fast*
  'to race' (the **verb**) is *always* fast

- *reckon* = 'think', 'decide'

- Connect the words: *gap, gape* and *gaping*.
  surf, surfboard and *windsurfing*.

SECTION 4 Access advert

Begin with a general discussion about buying and selling.

How often do members of the class... use credit cards, cheques or cash?
           ... barter?
Under what circumstances would these different forms of payment be appropriate?
Would you buy a newspaper with a credit card?
Would you pay cash for a palace?

Explain that the advert gives a list of some of the countries in which the Access credit card can be used.

The symbol of the company is a capital 'A' and this letter has been removed from the top half of the advert.

The joke is that without an 'A', you would be 'lost', either literally, in that you wouldn't know where you were, or metaphorically, in that you would be in problems without your card.

Divide the class into groups and then ask them to do three things. (This exercise will work much better if students have access to an atlas, globe or wall map.)

a Work out the full name of the sixty countries mentioned.
b Decide whether these countries are in Africa, Asia, the Caribbean, etc.
   (question **1** on page 63).
c See how many countries they can name that are not mentioned in the advert.

Check the answers, and then go through the text showing how very colloquial and conversational the language is.

Perhaps mention some of the following points:

- q*uite* can mean either.... 'fairly' ('quite good', 'quite easy').

  or (as here)   '100% ('quite impossible', 'quite frankly')

- *far and away* = 'much', 'a lot'

- *whatever* = it doesn't matter what (see pages 16-17)
- *whenever* = it doesn't matter when
- *wherever* = it doesn't matter where

- *the chances are that...* = 'it is probable that...'

Then complete questions **2** to **6,** before moving on to the follow-up questions (given below).

Answers:

1 South America   Uruguay, Ecuador, Venezuela, Colombia, Brazil,
                         Paraguay

Central America	Panama
North America	USA
Africa	Algeria, Chad, Zaire, Zimbabwe, Uganda, Swaziland, Gabon, Mauritius, Rwanda, Tunisia, Liberia
The Middle East	Bahrain, Kuwait, Jordan, Lebanon
Asia	India, Pakistan, Singapore, Sri Lanka, Thailand, Taiwan, Maldives
Scandinavia	Norway, Finland, Denmark, Iceland
The Caribbean	Barbados, Jamaica, Grenada, Bahamas, Dominica, Haiti, Cuba
Eastern Europe	Bulgaria, Hungary, Poland
Western Europe	Andorra, England, Scotland, Italy, Austria, Germany, Portugal, Malta, France, Spain, Scotland, Wales, Gibraltar
Australasia	Australia, Samoa

- Some countries could be put into more than one group, since Scandinavia is part of Western Europe and the Middle East is part of Asia, etc.

2 a large number of notes held together
3 a cheque that you can 'buy' in one country and 'cash' in another
4 the money used in a particular country – you change 'travellers cheques' into 'local currency' when you arrive.
5 more than 170
6 up to £350 worth of local currency

Follow-up discussion:

Are credit cards a good idea? Or do they encourage people to get into debt?

Will 'plastic money' replace 'cash'? Will we still be using coins and notes in a hundred years' time?

There are dozens of different currencies in the world. Is that a good idea?

When you have money, do you save it or spend it?

SECTION 5 Gerund words and expressions _____

Follow the same pattern that you used for the **infinitive words** and **infinitive expressions** on page 39.

Emphasise that a verb placed immediately after a **gerund word** or a **gerund expression** will always be in the gerund form.

Explain that *all* prepositions are **gerund words** and ask for or give examples.

eg. 'She talked me *into buying* a rusty secondhand car.'
  'She learned English *by listening* to the radio.'

The only problem with the above rule is the use of the word *to* which can be either:

a **preposition** (in which case it is followed by a verb in the **gerund** form)

or part of an **infinitive** (in which case, of course, it is followed by a verb in the **infinitive** form).

Among the many possible answers for these two exercises are:

Exercise 1

1 painting   4 stealing... forging
2 getting   5 shaving
3 going   6 losing

Exercise 2

1 reading
2 arguing
3 travelling
4 telling
5 skiing... swimming
6 buying

Notice how the noun and the gerund form of a verb are often spelt the same (eg. skiing, swimming, walking, writing, flying etc.). This is a point picked up in the blank-filling exercises of *Personal Passport*.

SECTION 6 Temporals and Conditionals

Start by considering how to form the **future tense**:

Either   *a*   *will* or *shall* + an infinitive

or   *b*   the **Present Continuous**

At this point, you may be asked to explain the difference between *will* and *shall*.

This is a very contentious and complex question and one on which grammar books disagree. However, I think there are two points you can make with reasonable safety.

1 Generally speaking, *shall* is only used with 'I' and 'we'.
2 When asking a question, *shall* indicates an **offer** or **suggestion**:

    'Shall I carry the bag for you?'
    'Shall we go out for a walk?'

whereas *will* is used when asking for **information:**

    'Will the shop be open tomorrow?'
    'At what time *will* the train arrive?'

Ask the class to consider the three sentences at the bottom of page 65. Here we express the future in a different way, with the **Present Simple** tense.

Go through the lists at the top of page 66, explaining the differences between a **temporal** and a **conditional** and asking for or giving examples for each word. Then ask students to do the exercise in pairs and go through the notes at the bottom of the page, pointing out the **key exception** to the above rule – the formation of a question beginning with the word *when*.

Answers:

1 I won't speak to her until she apologises.
2 I won't pay you unless you finish the job.
3 I'll get there as soon as I can.
4 I'll still love you whatever you do.
5 She'll check in an hour before the plane takes off.

6 They won't go swimming if the water is cold.
7 We'll wash up after the guests leave.
8 I'll take an umbrella in case it rains.
9 I'll fax you the document the moment I get to the office.
10 I'll pop over to see you when I have a day off.

SECTION 7 Reported (indirect) speech

There are several pages of close, detailed information here and you may like to divide up the four exercises, doing **reported speech** one day and **reported questions** the next.

REPORTED SPEECH

Go through the explanation at the top of the page, emphasising that 'A listens to B and then passes the information on to C'.

Then write a **board summary** of reported speech explaining how in this form you normally...

> 1 drop the inverted commas
> 2 paraphrase what was said
> 3 restructure the sentence
> 4 change the tense.

Go through the list at the bottom of page 67 in the student's book before setting and checking the exercise on page 68. (You will find the answers on page 47.)

REPORTING QUESTIONS

Consider first how to change questions formed with
  a the verb *to be*
  b the auxiliary *have* or *has* + **past participle.**

Write the six key changes up on the board:

> 1 the inverted commas are dropped
> 2 the inversion is dropped
> 3 the words spoken are paraphrased
> 4 *if* is normally added
> 5 the question mark is dropped
> 6 the tense is changed.

Then divide the class into pairs and ask them to prepare **Exercise 2**.

As you go through the answers, point out the six changes that have been made in each sentence.

Explain that changes **1, 3, 4, 5** and **6** are also made when reporting sentences that begin with *do, does* or *did*. However, point **2** does not apply because there is no inversion in the original sentence. So rub 'the inversion is dropped' off the board and replace it with a short explanation such as 'you drop *do, does* or *did*'.

Practise reporting *do/does/did* questions with a **cross-setting.** (See Introductory Notes, page 11.)

The use of would

Write sentences demonstrating the two meanings of *would* on the board.

eg. *a* 'Would you like a drink?
    b 'Would you make me a cup of tea?'

Underline the first word in each sentence and then ask if *would* has the same meaning in *a* and *b*.

Explain or elicit the fact that in *a*, *would* = an offer, whereas in *b*, *would* = a polite request.

Then explain how *would* can be reported in two separate ways depending on its meaning, and set and check the exercise at the bottom of the page.

Exercise 1

1 She said she was a doctor.
2 He said the children were watching TV.
3 The salesman said he would tell a white lie.
4 The policeman said he would do it the following (next) day.
5 The pilot said she had a problem.
6 She said she had won a silver medal at the 1956 Olympics.

Exercise 2

1 She asked me if the post office was open.
2 He asked me if I had seen the film.
3 She asked me if the mechanic had fixed the car.
4 They asked me if I was Spanish.

Exercise 3

1 She asked me if I wanted a drink.
2 She asked me to make her a cup of tea.
   She asked me if I would make her a cup of tea.
3 She asked me if I wanted to hear some music.
4 She asked me to sing a song for her.
   She asked me if I would sing a song for her.

Exercise 4

1 She asked me to explain it (to her) again.
2 She begged me not to tell him the secret.
3 The policewoman ordered us to leave the area immediately.
4 The soldier warned me not to touch that button.

SECTION 8 The Present Perfect _____

Perhaps start by drawing a line down the middle of the board and writing **Present Perfect** at the top of one column and **Simple Past** at the top of the other.
Then ask the class to explain the difference between the two tenses. As the various points are made, write them up under the appropriate headings.

You might end up with the board looking like this:

PRESENT PERFECT	SIMPLE PAST
1 action that has just happened 2 action completed at unspecified time (often used with *already* or *yet*) 3 action begun in the past and still continuing	1 action finished some time ago 2 action completed at specified time (eg. in 1989) 3 regular past action now ended

Start the exercise in pairs and then expand it out into a general class discussion. As you go through the answers, point to the appropriate explanations on the board.

This is a key grammar point and one that causes real confusion. So don't rush through it or skip any of the ten questions. The repetition built into the exercise is quite intentional.

SECTION 9 The Lion

Answers:

1 *d* in a specially designed trailer.
2 *b* at midday.
3 *c* is getting very hungry.
4 *c* have sealed off the centre of the town.

Michael Clarke: 'It's one o'clock and here is the lunchtime news from Radio Waverly. I'm Michael Clarke...
'Police have sealed off all main roads into Rochdale city centre as efforts continue to recapture a circus lion that escaped while being transported to the Sidwell City Zoo. The drama began just over an hour ago when a bus, a security van and a motorcycle were involved in a collision on the A3542 ring road. The pile-up caused a lorry pulling a specially designed animal trailer to swerve and run into the crash barrier. The bars of the trailer buckled on impact and Ambala – a three year old African lion – managed to wriggle its way free. The lion then ran into the Ferriston Valley Shopping Centre and, as hundreds of lunchtime shoppers fled in panic, police evacuated the area and sealed off neighbouring roads. We're now going live to the scene for this report from Tracey Dennis...'

Tracey Dennis: 'Good afternoon, Michael... Well, the latest news from here is that the lion is on the third floor of the shopping centre. It was first spotted in WH Smiths but it has now gone into the shoe department at Marks and Spencers. According to handlers from the Sidwell City Zoo, the lion hasn't eaten for five or six hours, so it's obviously getting very hungry and police are warning the public to stay well clear of the area. My understanding is that there are some twenty police officers at the scene and we're now waiting for a vet to arrive from Sidwell. The plan then is to try to immobilise the lion with a tranquilliser dart.

'But for the moment, the news from here is that all roads into Rochdale city centre have been sealed off and police are advising motorists to use alternative routes...
'This is Tracey Dennis on the second floor of the Ferriston Valley Shopping Centre...'

SECTION 10 The Children's Charter

This is a topic on which everyone has strongly subjective views based on years of personal experience, so don't be surprised if it generates a particularly fierce debate. Start the exercise at the beginning of a lesson so that if the discussion does take off, you'll have enough time to develop the issues properly.

Make sure everyone understands the difference between *must, should* and *ought to* and then divide the class into groups of four. Explain that the idea is to write a **Children's Charter** for the United Nations, defining ten basic principles as to how children should or shouldn't be brought up. Ask the groups to 'brainstorm' for a few minutes, jotting down thoughts at random. They will probably come up with more than ten ideas.

The next stage is to whittle this first draft down to make a final list of ten points. This may take quite a long time as there is bound to be some disagreement, not only over 'right' and 'wrong' answers, but also in terms of priorities.

Ask each group to read out their charter. Encourage the other members of the class to react to and comment on any of the contentious points. Then, if you have the time, ask the class to decide on a final charter incorporating the best ideas from all the various groups.

Encourage people to say *what* they believe and *why* they believe it.

Structure the discussion, but do also be flexible enough to 'go with the flow', developing themes as they come up.

From the teacher's point of view, classroom debates are notoriously difficult to organise because they normally end up as an exclusive discussion between the two or three people who happen to be in control of a particular set of facts. However, this topic is different because we are all 'experts', and this should give you the chance to involve every member of the class.

SECTION 11 *call*

SECTION 12 Phrasal verb story

Follow-up questions:

1 What did Frederick... run across?
                            crawl through?
                            wade through?
                            climb up?
                            run down?
                            slip through?
                            run down?
2 What thoughts were running through his mind when the blue Rolls Royce glided to a halt?

SECTION 1 'The Currency Traders'

SECTION 2 Vocabulary multiple choice

1	*c*	on	11	*d*	at
2	*c*	weight	12	*c*	fresh
3	*d*	skimmed	13	*d*	cereal
4	*c*	give	14	*a*	scales
5	*b*	down	15	*b*	potatoes
6	*a*	raw	16	*c*	white bread
7	*a*	sauce	17	*b*	recipes
8	*c*	cream	18	*c*	to
9	*b*	snack	19	*b*	keep-fit
10	*d*	hungry	20	*b*	slim

For questions such as **6, 7, 9, 10, 16, 17** and **20**, ask the class to compare the four words given.

> eg. What is the difference between 'underweight' and 'skinny', or between 'receipts' and 'prescriptions'?

SECTION 3 'Do you eat too much?'

B Vocabulary

1 clue
2 type
3 generally
4 boiled
5 definitely
6 snacks
7 growing
8 make a new start

C Comprehension

1 The top half of the advert features a garden fork and a shovel, tools used for heavy physical work. Perhaps the message is that most of us overload our bodies with unnecessary food.
2 food that contains a lot of fat
3 very full, about to explode
4 It contains less fat.
5 Jacket potatoes are baked in their skins in the oven.
   Boiled potatoes are peeled and then cooked in boiling water.
   Mashed potatoes are peeled, boiled and mashed with added butter, salt and pepper.
   Roast potatoes are peeled and cooked in oil in the oven.
   Chipped potatoes are peeled, sliced and then fried in oil.
6 The language is informal and conversational. The sentences are short, and use phrasal verbs and expressions like 'it's not the final word', 'give you a clue', 'bloated', and 'not a chance'.
   This is perhaps to make the advert sound like a friend giving you advice, as it

might make more of an impact that way.

E Pair work

The structure of this exercise is very simple – just two people talking about what they eat and then deciding whether this constitutes a good or bad diet. But the conversation in pairs and subsequent class discussion may become surprisingly involved so, as with the **Children's Charter,** give yourself enough time to develop the themes properly.

SECTION 4 Conditionals

Explain that the three basic conditionals have different forms and different meanings.

Prepare a **board summary** for page 81:

FIRST	**Present simple... Future Simple** (present or future)	something easy or probable
SECOND	**Simple Past... modal + infinitive** (present or future)	something difficult or unlikely
THIRD	**Past Perfect... modal + Present Perfect** (past)	what did or did not happen in the past

Then go through the rubric at the top of page 82 and play the tape twice, using the pause button as necessary. You will find students referring to the board while deciding *a* which of the three conditionals is being used and *b* why that particular form is appropriate.

Having checked the answers, point to the relevant area on the board and explain that there are other common forms of the conditional which are listed in the Reference Section at the back of the book.

1 If you help me, I'll help you. (FIRST)
2 If she wins the race, she'll earn a lot of money. (FIRST)
3 If he won the race, I'd be very surprised. (SECOND)
4 If she had won the race, she would have earned a lot of money. (THIRD)
5 If you give me your address, I'll send you a postcard. (FIRST)
6 If you gave me a million pounds, I would be very happy. (SECOND)
7 If you had paid the fine, they wouldn't have put you in jail. (THIRD)
8 If you take these pills, you'll feel better in the morning. (FIRST)
9 If you had taken my advice, you wouldn't have got into this mess. (THIRD)
10 If you eat all those sweets, you'll get indigestion. (FIRST)
11 If I won the state lottery, I'd buy an island in the Caribbean. (SECOND)
12 If you cook the food, I'll wash up... OK? (FIRST)
13 If I see her, I'll give her your message. (FIRST)
14 If you had told me you were a vegetarian, I wouldn't have cooked Irish stew. (THIRD)
15 If you scratch my back, I'll scratch yours. (FIRST)

SECTION 5 Children and the law

True/false questions are a common feature of Paper 4 and ideal for **cross-setting**.

'PG' = Parental Guidance

The main film categories in Britain are:

U (Unclassified) → can be seen by anyone;

PG → can be seen by anyone aged 5 years and over, but parents are advised that the film may contain certain scenes that they might not want their children to see;

15 → can be seen by anyone aged 15 and over;

18 → can be seen by anyone aged 18 and over.

Answers:

1 true; 2 true; 3 true; 4 false; 5 false; 6 true; 7 true; 8 false; 9 true; 10 false; 11 true; 12 false.

Interviewer:	This morning I'm joined by Anthony Tomlinson, whose new book *Children and the Law* is published today. Anthony, you say in your introduction that the concept of legal rights for children is relatively new.
Anthony Tomlinson:	Yes. It wasn't until the late nineteenth century that children began to have what we would consider to be normal legal rights. Before then, the law was very vague and open to all sorts of interpretation and abuse. Children were often treated like slaves or animals. They were sent down the mines or forced to work fourteen hours a day in a factory and so on... The idea that a child had certain 'rights' would have been laughed at.
Interviewer:	And so when did this situation start to change?
Anthony Tomlinson:	Well, I think it's in the 1880s and 1890s that you begin to see significant changes in social attitudes towards children, and over the last hundred years, they have gradually been given more and more specific rights and freedoms. These days, the law is very clear about what a child can and cannot do.
Interviewer:	So what are the main points you'd mention?
Anthony Tomlinson:	Well, as far as the law is concerned, there are some things that children can do at any age. They can borrow money, open a bank account, give evidence in a court or choose their religion. You begin to have some additional rights from the age of five, when you can see a PG film unaccompanied, for example. And then at ten you are considered old enough to understand the difference between right and wrong. So if you break the law at this age, you can't say you were too young to know what you were doing. This, of course, has very wide-ranging implications and it means that a ten year old child can be taken into custody, fingerprinted, searched, detained or even

convicted of a criminal offence.

On a slightly happier note, at the age of twelve, you can buy a pet, and at thirteen, work for up to two hours a day at certain jobs, such as delivering newspapers. At fourteen, you can enter a pub, but not drink alcohol. At fifteen, you can see a category 15 film. And then at sixteen – when you become what some people call a 'young adult' – you can leave home, leave school, work full-time, get married (although you would still need parental consent at this age). You can join a trade union, claim supplementary benefit, apply for a passport and drive a moped.

Interviewer: Well, that's quite a range! What about seventeen?

Anthony Tomlinson: At seventeen, you can drive a car, become a street trader, get a pilot's licence, and be sent to prison.
And at eighteen, you are, to all intents and purposes, an adult. There are very few things you can't do by then. You are not allowed to be an MP or a local councillor, for example, and you can't hold a Heavy Goods Vehicle licence but, generally speaking, you have full legal and social rights.

Interviewer: I wonder what the Victorians would have made of all that? Thank you, Anthony, and good luck with the book – *Children and the Law* – which is published today by Hodder and Stoughton at £14.95.
My next guest...

SECTION 6 Comparatives

Comparatives and superlatives are practised in the Order of Size exercise on page 124.

SECTION 7 The apostrophe

1 the student's book = one student, one book
the student's books = one student, more than one book
the students' book = more than one student, one book
the students' books = more than one student, more than one book
2 the chemist = a person
the chemist's = a shop
3 My horse is bigger than Jane. = Jane is smaller than my horse.
My horse is bigger than Jane's. = Jane's horse is smaller than my horse.
4 She's already left. = She has already left.
She's leaving now. = She is leaving now.
5 I'd spoken to her before he arrived. = I had spoken to her before he arrived.
I'd like to speak to her before he arrives. = I would like to speak to her before
                                                    he arrives.

SECTION 8 The past

SECTION 9 Superlatives

See the Order of Size exercise on page 124.

SECTION 10 Phrasal verb story

Follow-up questions:

1 What caused the slow puncture?
2 Describe how Frederick changed the wheel.
3 Why did Frederick hold out his hand?
4 What suddenly dawned on him?
5 What did Lady Prescott put on?
6 What did Lady Prescott take off?

SECTION 1 'The Round Table'

SECTION 2 Vocabulary multiple choice

1	*c*	range	11	*d*	earn
2	*a*	book	12	*a*	income tax
3	*d*	cheque	13	*d*	take home
4	*a*	current	14	*d*	mortgage
5	*d*	rainy	15	*c*	hire
6	*a*	standing	16	*b*	meet
7	*c*	statement	17	*d*	so much
8	*b*	the black	18	*b*	branch
9	*a*	the red	19	*c*	overdraft
10	*c*	transaction	20	*b*	bounced

For questions **4** and **5,** contrast *current account* and *deposit account.*

VAT = Value Added Tax

Perhaps compare a 'direct tax', an 'indirect tax' and a 'duty'.

Ask the class about the tax system in their country.

Who pays tax?
How is it collected?
What percentage of your income do you pay tax on?
Should taxes be high or low? Why?

• For question **17,** *money* is uncountable.

SECTION 3 Midland Care Card advert

This is another advert for a credit card, but it has a very different style from the 'Access – where would you be without your A?' campaign on page 63.

Perhaps start with some general questions:

What differences can you see between the two adverts?
Are they aimed at the same kind of 'audience'?
Do they appeal to different emotions in us?

Explain the difference between the uncountable noun *charity* (= 'kindness', 'compassion') and the countable noun *a charity* (= 'an organisation').

A Comprehension

1 *d* throughout the world.
2 *d* the bank will donate £5 to the charity of your choice.
3 *c* the bank will donate 25p to the charity of your choice.
4 *a* is a telephone number.
5 *b* is made of plastic.

Unit 7

SECTION 4 Charities

Answers:

1	Age Concern	works in conjunction with local authorities to provide such services as 'meals on wheels', 'day care centres' and social clubs for the elderly.
2	The St John's Ambulance Brigade	provides volunteer First Aid services at major public events.
3	The Terrence Higgins Trust	gives advice and information about AIDS.
4	The NSPCC	helps children that have been neglected or ill-treated.
5	The Royal National Institute for the Blind	runs the highly successful 'Talking Book' scheme.
6	The British Diabetic Society	believes that new research into insulin will have a major impact on the treatment of diabetes.
7	The Royal National Institute for the Deaf	helped to persuade the BBC and ITV to add teletext subtitles to popular TV programmes.
8	The Spastics Society	develops educational programmes for people suffering from cerebral palsy.

Customer: Good morning. I saw your advert about the care card just recently in the paper and I wonder if you can give me some more information about the various charities involved?

Bank Clerk: Ah, yes, of course. At the moment there are twelve different organisations receiving donations. I suppose the one that's the best known is the NSPCC – that's the National Society for the Prevention of Cruelty to Children. As you may know, their main aim is to protect children who are at risk from violence or abuse. They also help children that have been neglected or ill-treated in some way. Then there's the St John's Ambulance Brigade. Their volunteers provide First Aid services at major public events – pop concerts, demonstrations, football matches and so on. The Terrence Higgins Trust is a fairly new charity. It was established in 1988. They give advice and information about AIDS. They have a 24-hour hotline and you can ring up at any time, day or night, and talk to a counsellor or get confidential advice...Another charity involved in the scheme is The Royal National Institute for the Blind. They run a scheme called the 'The Talking Book', the idea being that they've put hundreds of stories and plays onto cassette and distribute these by post to all parts of the country. The Spastics Society develops educational programmes for people suffering from cerebral palsy. They have specialist schools which have produced some extraordinary results in the past few years... Then there's the Royal National Institute for the Deaf. Their equivalent scheme to the 'Talking Book' project for the blind has been to persuade the BBC and ITV to provide teletext subtitles for popular TV programmes... The charity Age Concern is also involved in the scheme. Their staff work in conjunction with local authorities to provide welfare services for the elderly. They include things such as day care centres, social clubs

and 'meals on wheels', which runs a door-to-door delivery service of ready-cooked meals to people who are unable to cook their own... Another one is The British Diabetic Society. Now, that organisation strongly believes that new research into insulin will have a major impact on the treatment of diabetes, and, consequently, they have been very influential in this area... Then there's the, erm...
(fade)

The four other charities that benefit from the Midland Care Card are The Cancer Research Campaign, The British Red Cross, The Multiple Sclerosis Society and The Save The Children Fund.

SECTION 5 Writing a summary

Exercise 2

For pair or group work.

You can make this exercise more challenging by changing the rubric of the question and asking students to re-write the story in *exactly* 180 words, not a syllable more nor a syllable less. This means that after the pairs/groups have written their first draft, they have to 'fine tune' the text so as to adjust it to the exact figure of 180 words. This second phase may take as long as the first.

Personal Passport gives detailed guidance on how to write a narrative for Paper 2 and quotes examples from the Frank Pepperton story on pages 95 and 96.

SECTION 6 Adverbs of frequency

Do a **board summary** of page 97:

---

1 after verb *to be*
2 between **auxiliary** and its **verb**
3 before a **main verb**

Exception: *has/have/had...* **adverb of frequency**... *been*

Answers:

1 I have *never* eaten Indonesian food.
2 I *often* go to the cinema.
3 He is *always* bad-tempered early in the morning.
4 She *never* complains about my cooking.
5 She is *always* complaining about my cooking.
6 He *occasionally* missed a lesson.
   He missed a lesson *occasionally*.
   Occasionally he missed a lesson.
7 He has *occasionally* missed a lesson.
   Occasionally he has missed a lesson.
   He has missed a lesson *occasionally*.
8 He was *occasionally* late for the lesson.
   Occasionally he was late for the lesson.
   He was late for the lesson *occasionally*.

9 She has *never* forgiven me.
10 I *often* think about you.
11 Have you *ever* been there?
12 He's *never* been to Ireland.
13 I *always* sing in the bath.

Exercise 2

Among the many possible answers for this exercise are:

1 How often do you shave?
2 How often do you go swimming?
3 How often do you wash your hair?
4 How often do they eat out?
5 How often do they pay you?
6 How often do you see a snowstorm in the desert?
7 How often does the comet appear?
8 How often do you eat sweets?

Exercise 3

The Totally Truthful Travel Company

This exercise can be done in two ways, depending on the type of class you are teaching. If you are using the book with a single nationality class, ask them to describe their own country. If, however, you have a mixed nationality group, ask them to describe the country they are studying in.

Emphasise the fact that
    a they should use as many **adverbs of frequency** as possible
and
    b the Totally Truthful Travel Company will not publish lies, exaggerations, half-truths or propaganda, so the descriptions must be absolutely honest.

Go round helping with vocabulary, grammar and presentation, and then ask one member of each group to read out their report.

SECTION 7 *must be/might be/can't be*

Go through the three model sentences at the top of page 99 and clarify the differences between the three forms. Give extra examples if necessary.

Emphasise that the five friends all have different jobs, different interests and different ages. Then explain how the grid on page 100 works (perhaps getting students to mark in the information given on page 99-100) and start the exercise in pairs.

This is an unusual and complex activity, so it's a good idea to go around the pairs clarifying the procedure.

After ten minutes or so, review how the exercise is going. If the pairs are working well, just let them continue. If, however, some are finding it difficult, join two pairs together into a group of four, suggesting that they should compare notes and then carry on together.

Answers:

Name	Age	Occupation	Favourite Sport
Colin	54	journalist	squash
Angela	52	pilot	cricket
Tom	50	plumber	skiing
Sandra	48	dentist	golf
Andrew	46	teacher	tennis

SECTION 8 *wish*

Emphasise that *wish to* is more formal than *want to* or *would like to*, and perhaps write a **board summary** along the lines of:

1 *wish to*	= want to, would like to
2 *wish...* (pro)noun... simple past	= regret about the present
3 *wish...* (pro)noun... past perfect	= regret about the past

Then set the exercise.

When checking the answers, clarify the tenses used. Many students find it difficult to grasp the fact that you use a **Simple Past** when describing the present and a **Past Perfect** to describe a single action in the past.

You might like to explain that the *'wish...* (pro)noun... verb' form describes something impossible or unalterable and is considered by some to be a kind of **subjunctive**, hence the odd tense construction.

Or you could link up similar 'past describing present' forms such as:

'It's time you got a job...'
'It's about time you got a job...'
'It's high time you got a job...'
'I'd rather you didn't sit on my white settee with dirty trousers.'

Answers:

1 I wish to learn Spanish.
2 I wish I was fit.
3 I wish I hadn't bought a house with rising damp.
4 I wish I hadn't stolen her purse.
5 I wish I had gone to the party.
6 I wish I hadn't told her a lie.
7 I wish she wasn't so moody.
8 I wish I was creative.
9 I wish I could play the piano.
10 I wish I could swim.
11 I wish I had taken your advice.
12 I wish I hadn't taken your advice.

Group Exercise

Divide the class into groups of six or seven. Ask everyone to take a blank sheet of paper and write down five personal sentences, each beginning with the words 'I wish'. Then ask one member of the group to collect the papers, shuffle them, pin them together, and exchange them for those of another group.

Each group now has a bundle of six or seven sheets written by the other group. Based on what they know about their classmates, can they now work out who wrote which list?

• The photograph on page 102 is from an advert for Polaroid cameras.

SECTION 9 *used to/to be used to/to get used to* _____

This is one of the three or four most difficult grammar points in the book and you might like to come back to it more than once.

Write a **board summary** of the explanations on page 103 along the lines of:

1	*used to*	+ **infinitive**	regular past action, now ended
2	*to be used to*	+ **gerund**	something normal, regular, familiar
3	*to get used to*	+ **gerund**	something unfamiliar ➤ something familiar

Then set the exercise. When going through the answers, emphasise three things:

   a the **infinitive** in type 1 sentences
   b the verb *to be* in type 2 sentences
   c the use of *get* in type 3 sentences.

Possible answers to the exercise include:

1	play	5	driving in the city
2	watch	6	telling
3	eat	7	working
4	ironing	8	living

SECTION 10 Phrasal verb story _____

• *Well I never!* = 'That's incredible!'

Follow-up questions:

1 What ran down Frederick's spine?
2 Who was getting carried away?
3 Why is Sir Gerald called Niagara?
4 What had the 'tiger' turned into?
5 Why was Frederick's mind not at peace?

SECTION 1 The boy and the elephant' ————————

SECTION 2 Vocabulary multiple choice ————————

1	*a*	since	14	*b*	sheep
2	*c*	rising	15	*c*	jumpers
3	*a*	milk	16	*d*	harvests
4	*a*	feeds	17	*b*	mill
5	*b*	rides	18	*c*	ploughs
6	*b*	chops	19	*a*	sows
7	*a*	logs	20	*a*	plants
8	*a*	yard	21	*b*	barn
9	*d*	broom	22	*b*	simple
10	*c*	cleans	23	*b*	wouldn't
11	*c*	scrubbing	24	*a*	living
12	*c*	lights	25	*d*	of
13	*a*	dusts			

For number **2**, explain that 'at the crack of dawn' means 'as dawn breaks.'

Raise and *rise* are discussed on page 123.

For questions **5, 7, 10, 11** and **18**, elicit or explain the differences between the four possible answers.

SECTION 3 'Boy, 7, yanks out five teeth...' ————————

B Vocabulary

1	gap	6	crept
2	every	7	neatly
3	furious	8	proper
4	stuck to	9	giggled
5	bargain	10	putting in

C Comprehension

1 false; **2** false; **3** true; **4** false; **5** true; **6** false; **7** true; **8** false; **9** false; **10** true.

SECTION 4 The Tooth Fairy ————————

As the class are listening to the tape for the first time, follow the pattern outlined in the Introductory Notes on page 11.

Answers:

1 toothbrushes
2 1600... six... sixty.
3 79%... 81%... 80%... 78%... 81%...
4 four out of five
5 *a* tissue
   b wall... family
   c glass

Unit 8

61

d carpet
e put the tooth under the bed.
6 even more... fifty

Alan:	What are you reading?
Susan:	It's an article about the tooth fairy.
Alan:	Susan, hold on, the tooth fairy doesn't exist.
Susan:	Doesn't it? Another of my illusions gone... No, this is about a market research survey that they did for WISDOM – you know, the company that makes toothbrushes. You see, WISDOM are just about to launch a new range of toothbrushes for children and they wanted to find out if kids were still told the story of the tooth fairy. Anyway, what they did was to interview 1600 people, aged six to sixty, and they asked the children if they believed in the tooth fairy and they asked the adults if they knew of any particular local traditions connected with children losing teeth.
Alan:	And what did they come up with?
Susan:	Well, the first thing they discovered was that four out of five children believe the story and as a result, very few teeth get thrown away. In fact, they've got a list here, region by region, of the number of children who leave a lost tooth under a pillow.
Alan:	So what are the figures?
Susan:	In London and the South East, it's 79%. In Wales and the West Country, it's 81%. In the East Midlands, it's 80%. In the North of England 78% and in Scotland, it's 81%.
Alan:	So, it's about the same everywhere.
Susan:	Yeah, it seems so...
Alan:	And what else did they find out?
Susan:	Well, apparently there are all sorts of traditions in different parts of the country. In the East Midlands, it's customary to wrap the tooth in tissue before you place it under the pillow. In London, some children throw the tooth over a wall and if you hear the tooth land, this means you are going to have a large family... In Wales and the West Country, they put the tooth in a glass. And children in the North of England might also put the tooth under a carpet. And then in Scotland, children place the tooth under a bed. At the end of the article, they say that WISDOM did a similar survey to this fifty years ago and when you compare the two reports, it seems that the tradition of the tooth fairy is even more popular now than it was then.
Alan:	You know, it's strange, isn't it? You'd think in an age of TV and satellites and videos, children wouldn't believe in that kind of story any more.
Susan:	Well, maybe they don't. I mean, there aren't many easier ways of earning money, are there? Perhaps...
(fade)	

SECTION 5 Ladybird

1. on a door
2. at the front of a car
3. at an airport
4. on a beach
5. in a pack of cards
6. on a motorway
7. on a main road
8. in a hospital
9. on the outside of a building
10. in a washing room
11. in a kitchen
12. in sand, mud or fresh cement
13. on a door
14. at the bottom of the sea
15. in a garden, park or street
16. on a seat, sofa or armchair
17. in (long) hair
18. on the seashore
19. near rocks
20. far from inhabited land

SECTION 6 The advertising game

Don't worry if this exercise begins slowly. It will take some time for the group to orientate themselves and to work out what to do. Creating an advert involves **thinking, planning, designing** and **drawing,** so don't expect forty-five minutes of constant talking.

When the groups present their ideas, ask them to give details of the price, ingredients and packaging, plus their underlying 'market strategy'.

Encourage the groups to *a* add sound effects to their radio advert;
b describe the music they might use in the TV advert.

SECTION 7 Active and passive

Exercise 1

Explain how the **subject** of a sentence is normally more important than the **object** and, therefore, an **active** and a **passive** are emphasising different things.

When you write the answers to this exercise up on the board, underline
  a the verb *to be*
  b the **past participle.**

Emphasise the frequent use of a preposition (normally 'by') after the **passive** form.

Answers:

1. 'War and Peace' was written by Tolstoy.
2. The postman was bitten by the dog.

3 The hotel is run by Mr Edison.
4 'Sunflowers' was painted by Vincent Van Gogh.
5 The festival was sponsored by an oil company.
6 The fish was cooked in oil.
7 Mickey Mouse was created by Walt Disney.
8 The land was bought by an Australian businessman.

For questions **5** and **6,** point out the two different meanings of *oil*.

When explaining the Passive form of the **Present Continuous** and the **Past Continuous**, emphasise how the verb *to be* appears as two words:

   is/are/was/were   +   being

Exercise 2

1	Three new shopping centres are being built.	(by the company)
2	The bathroom and the kitchen have already been painted.	(by me)
3	When I arrived, the table was being laid.	(by them)
4	The book will be published next week.	(by them)
5	All the doors had been locked.	(by the night watchman)
6	Five meetings are being held next month.	(by them)
7	The play was being performed twice a day.	(by them)
8	The information will be faxed to you tomorrow morning.	(by me)
9	By the time the police arrived, the jewels had been stolen.	(by them)
10	Six Marilyn Monroe films are being shown next week.	(by them)

You might like to explain that in spoken English, we normally drop the agent ('by me', 'by them', etc.). In the exam, however, it's advisable to include it.

SECTION 8 *over-/under-*

1	overslept	8	overdose
2	underestimate	9	underprivileged
3	overcharged	10	overcooked
4	underpaid and overworked	11	overweight
5	overreacted	12	underdeveloped
6	overflowed	13	overtime
7	underdone	14	undernourished

In question **2**, point out the use of *much* with the comparative (eg. 'much cleverer').

In question **4**, contrast a 'day off' with an 'off day'.

In question **10**, note the **Present Perfect Continuous**. As explained on page 72 of the student's book, this tense emphasises that something has been going on non-stop over an extended period of time. The speaker is implying that the action has been going on too long.

SECTION 9 Phrasal verb cartoon

Follow-up questions:

1 Describe the area that Lady Prescott grew up in.
2 What did she put on?

3 What did she take off?
4 What happens when there is an election?

SECTION 10 Phrasal verb text

Follow-up questions:

1 Why did Lady Prescott leave her home town?
2 Where was the take-away?
3 What happened when her father found out what was going on?
4 What did she put on?
5 What did she make up?

SECTION 1 'Mist'

SECTION 2 Vocabulary multiple choice

1 *c*	sore	**11** *d*	in
2 *b*	high	**12** *c*	prescription
3 *c*	runny	**13** *a*	chemist's
4 *d*	down	**14** *b*	off
5 *c*	had	**15** *d*	easy
6 *d*	hot	**16** *c*	at
7 *a*	blankets	**17** *b*	feel
8 *b*	pills	**18** *c*	boss
9 *b*	cough	**19** *d*	over
10 *b*	tissues	**20** *d*	shelves

In question **2,** why is a temperature *high* rather than 'large' or 'tall'?

The answer has to do with convention rather than logic.
Like all languages, English is full of **collocations** (that is, pairs or chains of words that seem to fit together naturally).

These collocations are standard usage, but because they don't always make sense,
  a the student has to learn each one individually
  b you, as a teacher, have no rational answer to explain why one word is right and another wrong.

So it's a good idea to introduce the concept of collocations early on in a course, perhaps suggesting that students build up their own personal lists similar to those found in *Personal Passport*.

In question **4,** *'flu* = influenza

In question **17,** *until* is a temporal, so the future is expressed through a **Simple Present.**

SECTION 3 'Abominable snowstorm...'

• This article first appeared in *Today*.

Contrast 'to skid' and 'to ski'.

Poor can mean 'inadequate', as in 'poor visibility', 'poor eyesight', 'a poor answer', etc.

A *score* = 20 (eg. dozens of...scores of... hundreds of... thousands of...' etc.).

Connect 'a plough' and 'a snow plough'.

For *eight-mile tailback,* explain how all adjectives are singular in English, even those expressing a plural idea.

Explain the difference between *hold, grip, grab* and *grasp.*

Contrast 'speed' as a **noun** (which can refer to *slow* or *fast* movement) with 'to speed' the verb, which means to go very quickly.

Unit 9

Note how *fleet* is the collective noun for cars, ambulances, ships and planes.

B Vocabulary

1 chaos, havoc	6 blizzards
2 slush	7 tailback
3 commuters	8 straight
4 eager	9 hit out at
5 bound for	10 stranded

C Comprehension

1 true; 2 false; 3 true; 4 false; 5 true; 6 false; 7 false; 8 false; 9 false; 10 true.

SECTION 4 *Have something done*

Write a board summary of the information on page 120, along the lines of:

1	2	3	4
subject	*have*	noun	Past Participle

...have something done... to you.
                    for you.
                    on your behalf.

Emphasise the fact that...

a there are four elements in a fixed order;
b this construction can be found in all tenses.

As with the Passive, the agent is not normally mentioned when this construction is used in spoken English. In the exam, however, it is advisable to include the agent in full.

Answers:

1	I had my hair cut.	(by the barber)
2	I had my blood pressure checked.	(by the doctor)
3	She will have her eyes tested.	(by the optician)
4	We had our new central heating installed.	(by the plumbers)
5	I am having my car re-sprayed.	(by the garage)
6	I had the prescription made up.	(by the chemist)
7	We had the computers repaired.	(by the engineers)
8	We had new locks put on all our doors.	(by a locksmith)
9	We had our luggage taken up to the room.	(by the hotel porter)
10	She had her car stolen.	(by someone)

In question **8**, connect 'locksmith', 'goldsmith', 'silversmith' and 'blacksmith'.

In question **9**, *luggage* is uncountable.

SECTION 5 Differences

SECTION 6 *else*

1 Nothing else
2 Everyone else
3 What else
4 Who else
5 or else
6 someone else's

7 Someone else
8 who else
9 everyone else's
10 Why else
11 when else
12 Everyone else

SECTION 7 *raise/rise*

Perhaps begin by revising the difference between a transitive and an intransitive verb.

Write a board summary of page 123, along the lines of:

raise	*raised*	*raised*	*raising*	=	*to lift*	**(transitive)**
	collocations: to raise a child					
		the alarm				
		money				
rise	*rose*	*risen*	*rising*	=	*to go up*	**(intransitive)**

Then emphasise the fact that *raise* is **transitive**, whereas *rise* is **intransitive.**

Answers:

1 rises
2 rising
3 raise
4 raised
5 rise

6 rose
7 raised
8 risen
9 raise
10 raise

As you go through the answers, point to the correct form on the board.

In question **4,** explain the difference between *bring up* and *grow up.*

In question **5,** point out that you can also *call in* a plumber, an expert or an engineer.

In question **10,** explain that *break out* (= 'begin') is used for fires, wars, civil wars, fighting, epidemics, disease etc. and that it always has a negative meaning.

SECTION 8 Size

This section can be done in pairs or in groups.

Answers:

	1	2	3	4	5
1	ant	hedgehog	wolf	giraffe	whale
2	pill	potato	saxophone	ferry	mountain
3	teaspoon	tablespoon	spade	shovel	bulldozer
4	pin	seahorse	lamp	lamb	palace
5	mosquito	mushroom	pillow	sheep	ship
6	pencil	hammer	umbrella	see-saw	van
7	seed	peach	typewriter	eagle	beach
8	grape	camera	owl	wheelbarrow	hotel
9	rib	peacock	yacht	stadium	ocean
10	eyelash	frog	cauliflower	kangaroo	jeep

This might be a good moment to revise comparatives and superlatives, putting expressions like 'bigger than', 'smaller than', 'not as big as', 'not nearly as big as', 'much smaller than', 'the biggest' and 'the smallest' up on the board.

There may be some disagreement about certain comparisons. For example, is a camera bigger than an owl? Or is a balloon bigger than a donkey? This depends, I suppose, on whether you are talking about a 'pocket camera', a 'movie camera', a 'party balloon' or a 'hot-air balloon'... This kind of fine discussion point can be quite interesting so long as there are only a few contentious issues.

The idea is now picked up on the tape and becomes a combined aural, written and communicative exercise.

Keep the original pairs or groups, and use the pause button as and when necessary.

Answers:

	1	2	3	4	5	6	7	8
11	wasp	tomato	brick	dictionary	horse	tram		
12	pin	pen	pan	ball	bell	bull		
13	moustache	sock	hippopotamus	waterfall	airport	planet		
14	egg	apple	kingfisher	grapefruit	balloon	donkey	forest	
15	leaf	apricot	chicken	trumpet	chimney	camel	rainbow	glider

• **cross-setting**

SECTION 9 Phrasal verb story

Follow-up questions:

1 Why did she turn him down?
2 Why did the passengers have to get off the bus and walk?
3 Why was her father so angry?
4 What did she do after the wedding ceremony was over?
5 Describe the young Gerald Prescott.
6 Describe the postman on his bike.
7 Why didn't Frederick have a penny on him?
8 Why was Lady Prescott worked up?

SECTION 1 'The Toy Stall'

SECTION 2 Vocabulary multiple choice

1	c	lose	12	a	sure
2	d	frying	13	d	wide
3	b	between	14	d	save up
4	d	night	15	c	all
5	a	every	16	b	charges
6	d	some	17	a	a
7	c	'flu	18	c	to give
8	c	better	19	b	wood
9	c	take	20	d	sweeps
10	a	in	21	a	with
11	b	work			

SECTION 3 'Found among the milk bottles...'

• This article first appeared in the *Daily Mirror*.

B Vocabulary

1	barely	6	below
2	naked	7	spotted
3	shivering	8	rushed
4	chill	9	pint-sized
5	plummeted	10	wonderful

SECTION 4 Countable and uncountable nouns

Exercise 1

1	is	4	is/was
2	was	5	was
3	is/was	6	is/was

Exercise 2

1	It	4	it
2	it	5	it
3	it	6	It

This exercise is trying to make one simple point, hence the repetition.

Exercise 3

Start the exercise in pairs and then go through the answers with the whole class.

For many students, this will be the first time that they have heard of a noun having a countable and an uncountable meaning.

SECTION 5 *lay/lie/lie*

Follow the same structure you used for *raise* and *rise*.

1	laid	**5**	lie
2	lying	**6**	lay
3	laid... lay	**7**	lie
4	laid	**8**	laid

SECTION 6 Prepositions

Among various possible answers are:

1	to	**8**	of
2	about	**9**	on
3	on	**10**	at
4	for	**11**	off
5	from	**12**	in
6	to	**13**	for
7	for	**14**	off

SECTION 7 *up*

1	blew up	**6**	used up
2	dressing up	**7**	eat up... drink up
3	bought up	**8**	tore up
4	fill up	**9**	mess up
5	beaten up	**10**	fed up

SECTION 8 The Touts

1 *b*   very tall and slim.
2 *d*   a bit nervous.
3 *d*   the 8 o'clock performance of Batman 3.
4 *b*   £15.00
5 *d*   gets very angry when people use a tout.

Christine:	Officer?
Policewoman:	Yes, madam.
Christine:	I want to make a complaint.
Policewoman:	About what, madam?
Christine:	I've just been ripped off by two touts on Leicester Square and I've lost fifteen quid.
Policewoman:	Right... Well, you'd better give me some details. Now, what happened exactly?

Christine: Well, we wanted to go and see the new Batman film. You know, Batman 3. And we were in the queue for the eight o'clock performance. Anyway, we'd been waiting there for about twenty minutes, I suppose, when these two guys came up to us, and one of them said, 'Are you waiting for Batman?' Well, I thought it was a bit of a silly question, but I said 'Yes! Why?' and he said 'Do you want a couple of tickets?' Well... I mean... you know... it was pouring with rain, it was cold, and there were lots of people in front of us in the queue and we might not have been able to get in... So I just jumped at it and said 'Yes, sure. How much do you want for them?' and he said, 'Fifteen quid the pair.' And that was it... We gave them the money and they just disappeared...

Anyway, to cut a long story short, we went off to have a cup of tea and when we came back – you know, for the film – we showed the tickets at the door and they wouldn't let us in... And we said, 'But we've got tickets,' and the guy said, 'But not the right ones'... Now, what had happened is that these two touts had sold us cheap tickets for the six o'clock performance of Batman 2 which was in another cinema five miles away... And so I said...

Policewoman: I think it might be a good idea if you described the touts to me, madam... What were they like?

Christine: Well, the first one was tall. He was a bit shabby. You know, his shirt was frayed. There were a couple of buttons missing. I notice these things. He hadn't shaved for a couple of days... He was slim... a bit bald... Erm... The other one was very smart... He had a suit on... with all the buttons... He had gold cufflinks... I remember that... He was short and he wore glasses... and he was very quiet... He didn't say a word... He was fidgeting all the time... he couldn't stand still. He was a bit nervous, you know, kept looking over his shoulder...

Policewoman: Well, I know most of the touts in Leicester Square but that description doesn't fit any of the regulars... Right, madam, let me just ask you one or two questions... Now the tout who did all the talking... Did he say the tickets were for Batman 3?

Christine: Er... no... Not in so many words... no.

Policewoman: And did he say that the tickets were for an eight o'clock performance?

Christine: Er... no.

Policewoman: And did he say they were for a particular cinema?

Christine: No... but I just presumed that –

Policewoman: Well, madam, technically the touts have done nothing wrong... They didn't lie to you. They just asked if you wanted tickets for Batman, and that is what they sold you... I agree that they were economical with the truth but they didn't break the law... And so there's nothing I can do... I'm afraid they saw you coming...

Christine: But that's ridiculous... I mean what about the cinema manager? I mean... surely he'd give us a refund or a couple of complimentary tickets?

Policewoman: I doubt it somehow... The manager's not very sympathetic to people who use touts... It's something that makes her really angry...

Christine:	So what can we do then?
Policewoman:	Well, the only thing I can suggest, madam, is that you join the queue, over there, for the ten o'clock performance... and if you see the touts again, come and get me... I am here for another hour... Other than that, there's nothing else I can do...

SECTION 9 The Horse Race

1 true;   **2** true;   **3** false;   **4** true;   **5** true;   **6** false;   **7** true;   **8** false;   **9** false;   **10** true.

Commentator:	...And they're into the final furlong now, and it's Out of the Blue from News Flash and Total Stranger. Then it's Burst Into Tears, Upside Down, Do Me A Favour, Banana Skin, Back to Front, Inside Out, What's the Problem and Welsh Rabbit... It's still Out of the Blue a length clear from News Flash with the favourite Burst into Tears now up into third... And with a hundred yards to go... it's Out of the Blue, News Flash, Burst Into Tears, Total Stranger – and What's the Problem making a storming run on the stands rail, but has he left it too late? ...And as they come up to the line, it's Out of the Blue just hanging on from Burst Into Tears with News Flash third, Total Stranger fourth and What's the Problem, Back to Front and Welsh Rabbit! ...And so the result of the Ladbroke Spring Cup is... First, number eighteen, Out of the Blue, ridden by Michael Hills, trained by Malcolm Pike and owned by Willie Carson. Second, number six, Burst Into Tears, ridden by Walter Swinburn, trained by George Ryan and owned by Henry Cecil. Third, number four, News Flash, ridden by Pat Eddery, trained by Carol Vordemann and owned by Mrs Cathy Thompson. And fourth, number fifteen, Total Stranger, ridden by Steve Cauthen, trained by Nathalie Mitchell and owned by Tony O'Neill.

SECTION 10 -less/-free

1 duty-free	**8** tasteless/tactless
2 harmless	**9** helpless
3 penniless	**10** trouble-free
4 lead-free	**11** carefree
5 priceless	**12** useless
6 painless	**13** tax-free
7 homeless	**14** brainless

Some grammar books suggest that *-less* means 'without something good'
   eg. useless, hopeless, homeless, penniless
whereas *-free* means 'without something bad'
   eg. tax-free, duty-free, lead-free, risk-free.

But if you are going to use this as a general rule for the class, bear in mind that there are several exceptions eg. harmless, painless, faultless etc.

SECTION 11 A phrasal verb story

As before, write a summary of the exercise on the board, along the lines of:

Begin with	1	'It was a cold night on the Scottish mountains...'
or	2	'Early one morning, the phone rang in my study...'
or	3	'At the age of four and a half, Abdul Shroprinski could speak six languages, compose piano concertos, pilot a plane and swim like a fish...'
continue with		a story that contains at least 12 phrasal verbs
and finish with		'And inside they found two potatoes and a guide book about Vienna'.

Go round the class while the stories are being written, checking that the phrasal verbs are being used correctly. If a group runs out of ideas, advise them to:

a look back at the previous chapters of the Angus Macpherson story
or *b* go through the phrasal verb exercises linked to the Reading Comprehensions
or *c* refer to the alphabetical listing in the Grammar Reference Section.

Make sure all the texts are right before they are sent to the other groups.

SECTION 12

A Describing and Drawing

This might be a good moment to revise the expressions used to describe different areas of the photograph (Unit 1, page 12).

B Ladybird

		WHEN	WHY
1	a phone book	when looking up a number	
2	a darkroom		to develop photographs
3	a pen name		to conceal your true identity
4	shorthand	when taking down notes	
5	a tea cloth		to dry dishes
6	a two-way radio		to keep in contact
7	a waiting room	before an appointment	
8	a clothes horse		to dry clothes
9	a pushchair		to take out a young child
10	a lifejacket	when you are forced into the sea	
11	a photocopier		to run off copies
12	a bottle opener		to open a bottle

SECTION 13 Phrasal verb story

Compare *sit up, sit at, sit down, sit back* and *sit on.*

Explain how *up* is often found in phrasal verbs connected with creativity or imagination,

eg. 'to come up with an idea', 'to think up', 'to dream up', 'to make up a story', 'to make up your mind'.

Contrast *stationery* and *stationary.*

SECTION 1 'The Chinese School'

SECTION 2 Vocabulary multiple choice

1 *a*	hook	**12** *c*	missed	
2 *b*	note	**13** *b*	wouldn't do	
3 *c*	part	**14** *d*	out of	
4 *c*	owe	**15** *a*	union	
5 *d*	dare	**16** *d*	plenty of	
6 *c*	grew up	**17** *c*	track	
7 *a*	peeled	**18** *b*	out of	
8 *b*	frying	**19** *c*	set	
9 *d*	took	**20** *a*	butterflies	
10 *c*	rinse	**21** *d*	off key	
11 *b*	line			

• Connect 'owe you money', 'owe you an explanation' and 'owe you an apology'.

SECTION 3 'Sorry darling, I just popped out...'

• This article first appeared in the *Daily Star*.

A Vocabulary

1 foundations
2 popped out
3 horrified
4 cracks
5 got back
6 surveyed
7 rubble
8 sort

Note the use of *strengthen* here. Explain how many verbs that begin or end with *-EN* mean 'to make' and are followed by an **adjective** or **comparative.**

> eg. Sugar *sweetens* tea.
> Please *ensure* that you bring your passport.

You will notice that most of these verbs are formed by adding *-EN* before or after an **adjective** (*broad*en, en*large*). However, there are other verbs which are formed by adding *-EN* to a noun (*strength*en, en*rage*).

Explain how *charge* can mean...

a	*ask for money*	'They charged me £50.00.'
b	*put energy into*	'to charge a battery'
c	*accuse of*	'They charged her with reckless driving.'
d	*attack*	'They charged the enemy line.'

B Comprehension

1 *b* while Clancy was digging.
2 *d* three rooms fell onto the floor below.
3 *b* a carpenter.
4 *a* professional builders are too expensive.

SECTION 4 Flags

Answers:

a Burkina Faso	*b* Yemen	*c* Cameroon	*d* Belgium
e Ghana	*f* Ethiopia	*g* Senegal	*h* Chad
i Hungary	*j* France	*k* Colombia	*l* Mauritius
m Mali	*n* Gabon	*o* Sierra Leone	*p* United Arab Emirates

Bill: Jack?

Jack: Yes, Bill.

Bill: I've just been speaking to Mr Morgan about that meeting this afternoon.

Jack: What, the one all those foreign ministers and ambassadors are coming to?

Bill: Yeah. Well, apparently, they set up the conference room last night. You know, with all the tables and place names and little flags and everything.

Jack: Yeah.

Bill: And then someone was in here this morning, cleaning and polishing. And they moved all the flags.

Jack: Yeah. So?

Bill: Well, Mr Morgan wants us to put them all back. You know, before the meeting.

Jack: Oh, right. But how do we know which flag is which?

Bill: Ah. Well, he thought of that, 'cos he's given us this chart here with all the names on and everything.

Jack: So what are we going to do?

Bill: I don't know.

Jack: Well, how about if you keep the chart and I can go round putting the flags up in the right place? All right?

Bill: Yeah, why not? So what's the first one then?

Jack: Well, the first one has got three horizontal stripes with red at the top, yellow in the middle and green at the bottom. And in the middle of the yellow stripe, there's a black star.

Bill: Three horizontal stripes... red, yellow, green and a black star... Oh, right. That's Ghana.

Jack: Ghana. Right. I'll just put the flag there. Now, the next one's got exactly the same design – three horizontal stripes and a star in the middle – but the colours are different. There's red at the top, white in the middle and black at the bottom.

Bill: And what colour's the star?

Jack: Er... green.

Bill: Red at the top... white in the middle... black at the bottom, and a green star. Right. I've got it. That's Yemen.

Jack: Yemen goes... there. Now, the next one's got green on the left, red in the middle and yellow on the right – with a yellow star.

Bill: Yellow on the right was that?

Jack: Yeah.

Bill: Green on the left?

Jack: Yeah.

Bill: Red in the middle?

Jack: Yeah.

Bill: Yellow star?

Jack: Yeah.

Bill: That's Cameroon.

Jack: Cameroon. So that goes there. Now, the next one's got green on the left,

	yellow in the middle and red on the right – oh, and a green star this time.
Bill:	Green, yellow, red... and a green star. Senegal, that is. They're almost the same those two, Cameroon and Senegal.
Jack:	Yeah, they are, aren't they? There's only one more with a star, and this one's got two horizontal stripes, with red at the top and green at the bottom, and a yellow star.
Bill:	Red... green... with a yellow star... Got it. That's Burkina Faso, that is.
Jack:	Right, so that's all the stars done! Now, why don't we do the ones with three vertical stripes?
Bill:	OK.
Jack:	The first one's got black on the left, yellow in the middle and red on the right.
Bill:	Let's just have a look... Black left, yellow middle, red right... That's Belgium, that is.
Jack:	Belgium... That goes there... Now, there's another one that looks really like Belgium: blue on the left, yellow in the middle and red on the right.
Bill:	Blue left, yellow middle, red right... erm... That's Chad.
Jack:	Right. So Chad goes... there. Now, this one's blue on the left, white in the middle and red on the right.
Bill:	Blue left, white middle, red right. Erm... France.
Jack:	That goes there then... Erm... green on the left, yellow in the middle and red on the right?
Bill:	Green left, yellow middle, red right. That's Mali.
Jack:	Right. We're half-way through now. All the others have horizontal stripes.
Bill:	How many?
Jack:	Three or four.
Bill:	Well, look. I tell you what. Let's do ones with three stripes first. What have you got?
Jack:	There's one here with red at the top, white in the middle and green at the bottom.
Bill:	Red, white, green is... Hungary.
Jack:	OK. The next one is yellow at the top, blue in the middle and red at the bottom.
Bill:	Yellow... blue... red... Ah, that's Colombia.
Jack:	Green at the top, white in the middle and blue at the bottom?
Bill:	Green... white... blue... That's Sierra Leone.
Jack:	Green at the top, yellow in the middle, and blue at the bottom...
Bill:	Green... yellow... blue... is... Gabon.
Jack:	And the last one with three horizontals is green at the top, yellow in the middle and red at the bottom.
Bill:	Green, yellow, red... Ethiopia... That's the lot is it?
Jack:	No, there are a couple more.
Bill:	Let's hear them then.
Jack:	The first one's got four blocks of colour. There's a red vertical stripe on the left-hand side and then there's these three horizontal stripes: green at the top, white in the middle and black at the bottom.
Bill:	Red vertical, then green white black horizontal. Right. United Arab Emirates, that's what you've got there.
Jack:	And this one's got four horizontal stripes: red at the top, and then blue and yellow, with green at the bottom.
Bill:	Ah, that's got to be Mauritius.
Jack:	Right, that's it then. Sixteen flags, sixteen seats. I reckon we did a good job there, Bill...

SECTION 5 My Uncle Theodore

Among the several possible answers are:

1	to	11	doing
2	bought	12	an
3	and	13	may/can/could
4	of	14	up
5	on	15	other
6	on	16	tightly
7	on	17	standing
8	out	18	if
9	later	19	of
10	on	20	gave/handed

SECTION 6 The forest game

As with all 'psychology games', this exercise has to be handled with some care, particularly when talking about the CUP and the WATER.

This is what the symbols are meant to represent:

FOREST = your general view of life

If the forest is sunlit and peaceful, you are an optimist who sees good in others. If, however, you describe a dark and frightening place with dangers lurking in every corner, you are more pessimistic and cynical.

PATH = your future

Someone who describes broad, sweeping pathways that cut straight through the forest may be more hopeful about the future than someone who describes a rocky, winding path that seems to lead nowhere.

CUP = your family

Some drink from a white cup full of hot soup. Others describe a dirty, cracked cup which they throw away.

KEY = knowledge

Some describe a rusty key which they throw away. Others carry the key with them and then use it to enter the house (society).

WATER = sexuality

HOUSE = society

For some the house is bright, exciting, alluring. For others, it is locked, bolted, inaccessible, gloomy, impenetrable.

WALL = death

Having explained what the symbols mean, ask the pairs to go back over what they said to each other and work out an interpretation.

Follow-up discussion:

How reliable are 'psychology games'?
Are they revealing? Funny? Nonsense? A waste of time?

What did you learn about your partner?
What did you learn about yourself?

The forest is dark and dangerous. It's full of wild animals and strange sounds. You could easily get lost there. The path is narrow and covered with rocks and weeds. As I walk along, I see a dirty cup. It's cracked and chipped at the edges. I pick it up and look at it. Then I get angry and throw it away. I carry on down the path and I see a large key made of gold. I pick it up and put it in my back pocket.

A few moments later, I come to a small river. The water is fresh and cool. I dive in and swim to the opposite bank. I feel much better now. I climb out of the water. Then I see a large house straight ahead. There are iron bars at all the windows and the doors are locked.

I take the gold key out of my pocket and open the front door. It's all very quiet. The house seems to be empty. I go into the kitchen and get some food out of the fridge. I sit down and start to eat. After a while I feel tired, so I stretch out on a sofa and fall asleep.

When I wake up, the house is very hot. I'm sweating and my shirt is wet. I stand up and run down a dark corridor. I unbolt the door and rush outside. Then, all of a sudden, I come face to face with a huge stone wall.

I look to the left and the right. There's no one about. For some reason, I decide to climb up the wall and see what's on the other side. The stones are rough and sharp and I cut my legs. It takes me ten minutes to reach the top. But when I get there, I can see something extraordinary.

Beyond the wall, there is a green field. It's summer time and the sheep are eating grass. In the far distance, there's a children's playground with swings and a brightly painted merry-go-round. I hear laughter and a brass band playing slightly out of tune...

Answers:

1 true;   **2** true;   **3** false;   **4** false;   **5** false;   **6** false;   **7** false;   **8** true;   **9** true;
10 false;   **11** false;   **12** false;   **13** true;   **14** false;   **15** false;   **16** false;   **17** true;   **18** false.

For question **10,** explain the two meanings of the word *bank*.

SECTION 7 'Starting school can be child's play'

• This article first appeared in *The Sun*.

A directed writing exercise can be done in a number of ways:

   a by lifting information directly from the text;
   b as a sentence by sentence paraphrase;
   c by re-writing the text in your own words;
   d as a combination of all three of the above.

Encourage students to underline the relevant words, phrases or sentences in the main text. This makes it easier to identify the information you need for each of the paragraphs.

As explained in *Personal Passport,* a directed writing exercise is often an extended reported speech exercise in disguise. So make sure that the necessary changes to tenses, noun forms, punctuation and word order have been made.

SECTION 8

Exercise 1

1 imagination
2 imaginative
3 recommended
4 recommendations
5 carefully

6 skilful
7 aggressive
8 beautifully
9 impossible
10 hot

Exercise 2

1 *I'm really looking forward* to going on holiday.
              to my holiday.
2 *If* you don't pay the bill, I'll sue you.
3 *She has* been working there for twenty-five years.
4 *He suggested* going to the cinema.
              that we could go to the cinema.
5 *Raspberries* are cheaper than strawberries.
              cost less than strawberries
              are not as expensive as strawberries.
6 *It took* (us) three hours to get to the airport.
7 *The policeman told* us to leave the area at once.
8 *It was such* a cold day that we stayed indoors.
9 *A new hospital* is being built (by them) in the city centre.
10 *You don't* have to pay the bill immediately.
              need to pay the bill immediately.

SECTION 9 *Take*

1 took *off*
2 taken *out* of
3 taken *over* by
4 took *down*
5 take the book *back*

SECTION 10 Exam practice: Paper 2

Add a suitable set book question for number **5.**

SECTION 11 Phrasal verb story

Follow-up questions:

1 What did Frederick do after he left the office?
2 Why was the cashier suspicious at first?
3 Who went through his account?
4 Describe the ceremony in the ward.

5 Describe the conversation between Frederick and the director of the bank.
6 Why didn't Frederick sign the letter?

SECTION 1 'The London Marathon'

SECTION 2 Vocabulary multiple choice

1 *d* on	14 *c* through
2 *a* set up	15 *c* for
3 *d* afford	16 *a* arguing
4 *b* shame	17 *c* so
5 *b* towards	18 *b* only
6 *c* live	19 *d* her to come
7 *c* on	20 *c* near
8 *a* fined	21 *a* wide
9 *d* running	22 *d* stand for
10 *d* didn't	23 *b* head or tail
11 *c* tell	24 *b* How
12 *b* sheep	25 *a* run over
13 *a* remember	

SECTION 3 Greenpeace

A

2 *Acid rain* is rainwater with a high acid content (due to industrial pollution).
3 an animal group that is at risk, close to extinction
4 'grow', 'develop', 'blossom'
5 *Insects* have six legs, eg. ant, wasp.
  Mammals feed their young on breast milk, eg. pig, rabbit.
  Reptiles are cold-blooded and lay eggs, eg. crocodile, tortoise.
6 The latter is one step higher on the evolutionary scale.
8 *ransacked* = used, abused and then abandoned.
  on the brink of = 'on the edge of'
  oasis = a calm, fertile area in the middle of a desert

SECTION 4 Blank filling

The blank filling exercise in the exam normally tests a wide range of grammar points – prepositions, adjectives, adverbs, phrasal verbs, tenses, collocations, articles etc. So encourage the class to include a similar variety of questions in the exercises they set.

SECTION 5 'Giovanna Amati: One fast woman'

• This article first appeared in the magazine *Cosmopolitan*.

Before setting the exercise, go through the phrasal verbs:

a ...she has *worked her way up* successive formulas.
b Giovanna *works out* every day...
c 'I do a lot of skipping to *build up* stamina...'
d '...that would make you *slow down*.'
e 'He must be there to *care for* me...'

Unit 12

SECTION 6 Exam practice: Paper 2 _____

Add a suitable set book question for number **5**.

SECTION 7 The wedding _____

Answers:

1   *a*   fine and sunny.
2   *c*   he got held up.
3   *b*   yellow.
4   *c*   The Round Table.
5   *c*   India.

Liz:	Nancy, how are you? Oh, it's great to see you.
Nancy:	I'm fine, Liz. Really well. And how are you?
Liz:	Fine. Oh, but I was really disappointed to miss your wedding. I'd been looking forward to it for ages, but, as you know, at the last moment they sent me off to that big sales conference in Austria. I just couldn't get out of it. It was such a pity, but there was nothing I could do. So, anyway, tell me. How did it go?
Nancy:	Well, first of all, we were really lucky with the weather. The week before it had been awful. We'd had thunder, lightning, snow, hail, sleet, the lot. But on the actual wedding day, it was perfect. Dry, sunny, hot. Just the way you want it to be. And it makes such a difference. It gets people in a good mood and they seem to enjoy the day much more... And the church looked gorgeous. They'd put blue and white ribbons on all the pews and the bridesmaids wore these soft yellow silk dresses. And there was a choir, and all Tom's family came over from Canada. Oh, it was just unbelievable...
Liz:	So, it all went fine. No last minute hitches.
Nancy:	Well, we had one minor drama. The best man turned up late because there were some roadworks on the motorway and he got stuck in this five-mile tailback. But he got there before the main ceremony started, so that worked out all right in the end.
Liz:	And where did you have the reception?
Nancy:	It was at a restaurant called The Round Table. Do you know it?
Liz:	No. Where is it?
Nancy:	Well, you know the Turnley Roundabout?
Liz:	Yeah.
Nancy:	You take the first left there.
Liz:	Aha.
Nancy:	And then you go on for about half a mile and you come to Burford.
Liz:	Right.
Nancy:	And you know that old-fashioned post office they've got there?
Liz:	The one with the three statues outside?
Nancy:	That's it. Well, the restaurant is just around the corner from there.
Liz:	Oh, right. And how many people came to the reception?
Nancy:	I don't know exactly. Around eighty, I suppose.
Liz:	And what about the honeymoon?
Nancy:	Well, we did a tour down the west coast of India. Daman, Bombay, Mangalore, Alleppey... I tell you, it's so beautiful down there. I can't wait to go back...
(fade)	

SECTION 8 Wedding anniversaries

Answers:

1 *b* 2 years.
2 *b* a bag or a pair of shoes.
3 *d* The crystal anniversary comes before the china anniversary.
4 *c* forty years.
5 *c* romantic.

Customer:	Good morning.
Shopkeeper:	Good morning, sir. And how can I help you?
Customer:	Erm, I want to buy a present for a wedding anniversary and, erm, I don't really know what to get. I was wondering whether you could suggest something?
Shopkeeper:	Well, sir. Might I ask how many years the couple have been married?
Customer:	Erm, I don't really know... Is that relevant?
Shopkeeper:	Oh, yes. That's the whole point of a wedding anniversary present. You give a different kind of gift each year.
Customer:	Erm, in what way?
Shopkeeper:	Well, sir. After you've been married for a year, you celebrate your 'paper' anniversary, so a suitable gift at that moment might be a book or tickets for the theatre.
Customer:	Because these things are made of paper?
Shopkeeper:	Yes, sir. That's the idea. And then after two years, you have your 'cotton' anniversary. I normally recommend a table cloth or a cotton jacket for this. The third anniversary is 'leather' – a bag or a pair of shoes perhaps for that. Erm, and the fourth is 'flowers and fruit', and so it goes on. Each year has its own name and character and type of gift... right up to the 'diamond' anniversary, which you celebrate after sixty years.
Customer:	With a diamond?
Shopkeeper:	Yes, sir. And so that's why I wanted to know how many years the couple in question have been married.
Customer:	Ah, now I understand. Well, to be honest, I'm not sure exactly... About twelve, I suppose. But it could be more...
Shopkeeper:	Well, let's have a think, sir. Twelve is silk, thirteen is lace, fourteen is ivory and fifteen is crystal. Now if you're not sure which anniversary they're celebrating, perhaps you'd better play it safe and cover all the options. Look, erm, I tell you what. Why don't you give them, er, a couple of silk scarves, er, some lace handkerchiefs, and a crystal vase with imitation ivory handles? That should keep them happy for a while.
Customer:	Yes... Perhaps. But how much would all that cost?
Shopkeeper:	Well, if sir would like something cheaper, I'm sure I could –
Customer:	Oh, no, no... On second thoughts, the er... scarves and the handkerchiefs and the crystal vase would be just fine...
Shopkeeper:	And, er, how are you paying, sir?
Customer:	Do you accept credit cards?
Shopkeeper:	Yes, of course.
	Right, sir. Here we are. If you could just sign there for me... Fine. Thank you. Now that's yours, that's mine... And here are your things...

Customer:	Thank you. Erm. As a matter of interest, what are the main anniversaries after crystal?
Shopkeeper:	After crystal? Well, er, china is twenty, silver is twenty-five. And then you've got pearl at thirty, coral at thirty-five, ruby, forty, sapphire, forty-five, gold of course at fifty, emerald at fifty-five, and then diamond – as we said – at sixty...
Customer:	And do many people still follow this kind of tradition? I mean, it's silly, isn't it?... A bit old fashioned...
Shopkeeper:	Well, we all have our personal view on that, sir. But speaking for myself, I find it all rather romantic... I mean...
(fade)	

SECTION 9 Pronunciation

SECTION 10 Phrasal verb story

Follow-up questions:

1 Why didn't Frederick tell the court what he'd done with the money?
2 Why did Frederick suddenly feel down?
3 What did Lady Prescott look up?
4 Why did Frederick nod off in the car?
5 Why did Frederick break out into a cold sweat?

SECTION 1 'The Skydivers'

SECTION 2 Vocabulary multiple choice

1	*a*	puppies	**14**	*a*	business
2	*d*	tell	**15**	*c*	a
3	*d*	of	**16**	*c*	out
4	*d*	afraid	**17**	*d*	Dutch
5	*a*	do	**18**	*c*	wait
6	*b*	could	**19**	*a*	on
7	*a*	loaves of bread	**20**	*d*	much too
8	*c*	grazing	**21**	*a*	teaspoon
9	*b*	up	**22**	*c*	takes after
10	*b*	chef	**23**	*b*	out of order
11	*b*	weigh	**24**	*b*	working
12	*c*	committed	**25**	*c*	Welsh
13	*d*	out			

Contrast *I'm afraid of* (= 'I'm frightened of...') in question **3** with *I'm afraid that* (= 'I'm sorry, but...') in question **4**.

to go Dutch = everyone pays for themselves

Welsh rarebit (sometimes written *rabbit*) = cheese on toast

SECTION 3 'Man-made bee leads dance of the hive'

• This article first appeared in the *Daily Telegraph*.

Prof = Professor

Answers:

1 *d* brings nectar to the hive.
2 *c* by a mixture of sound and movement.
3 *a* did not imitate some of the sounds of a real bee.
4 *b* does not expect apiarists to use robot bees.

SECTION 4

group one	bacon	butter	coffee	eggs	jam	(breakfast)
group two	ball	court	net	racket	umpire	(tennis)
group three	bride	groom	reception	ring	toast	(wedding)
group four	clause	letter	paragraph	phrase	word	(language)
group five	judge	jury	lawyer	sentence	trial	(the law)

There are three 'red herrings' that could fit into more than one group – *court, sentence* and *toast*.

• **cross-setting**

Unit 13

SECTION 5 'Some people do, and some people don't'

- This article first appeared in the *Independent*.

SECTION 6 Sign language

Before playing the tape for the first time, it might be a good idea to teach the following words and expressions:

palm	little finger	curved
fist	ring finger	straight
fingertip	middle finger	at right angles to
	index finger	
	thumb	

Mandy Cooke:	If you look at the chart, you can see the signs we use for the twenty-six letters of the alphabet.
Sam Kennedy:	Right.
Mandy Cooke:	Now, we've labelled some of the signs: the ones for *A, B, D, E, I, K, L, Q, R, T* and *U*.
Sam Kennedy:	Aha.
Mandy Cooke:	But we haven't labelled the others.
Sam Kennedy:	Right.
Mandy Cooke:	So what we're going to do is this. I'm going to describe the signs for the fourteen missing letters – *C, F, G, H, J, M, N, O, P, S, V, W, X* and *Z* – and I'd like you to try and work out which sign is which letter, and then complete the chart. OK?
Sam Kennedy:	Yep.
Mandy Cooke:	Right. Let's start with *C*. For *C* you make a curved shape with the thumb and index finger of your right hand.
Sam Kennedy:	In fact, it's like a back-to-front *C* pointing in the wrong direction...
Mandy Cooke:	Yes, that's it. So you can add *C* to the chart.
Sam Kennedy:	OK.
Mandy Cooke:	And we can go on to *J*. Now, for *J* you put the index finger of your right hand on the tip of the middle finger of your left hand.
Sam Kennedy:	Index right on middle left. Erm... aha.
Mandy Cooke:	Then you 'draw' a letter *J*, taking the right index finger down across the palm and then under and around the thumb.
Sam Kennedy:	Hm. There are some dotted lines and an arrow on the chart.
Mandy Cooke:	Yes, that's the one.
Sam Kennedy:	Right, got it.
Mandy Cooke:	Now, *P*. This one's a bit more difficult to describe. You make a circle with the thumb and index finger of your right hand and you put that circle on the tip of the index finger of your left hand.
Sam Kennedy:	So, it's circle and left index... Yep.
Mandy Cooke:	Clear so far?
Sam Kennedy:	Yes, I think so.
Mandy Cooke:	Right, for *V* you make a *V* shape with the index finger and the middle finger of your right hand, and you put that against the palm of your left hand.
Sam Kennedy:	Aha.

Mandy Cooke:	And for *X*, you put the index finger of your right hand across the index finger of your left hand.
Sam Kennedy:	Making an *X*.
Mandy Cooke:	Exactly. Now, you may have noticed that with *C, J, P, V* and *X* you make a sign that looks like the letter.
Sam Kennedy:	Right.
Mandy Cooke:	But it's very often the case that you can't really recognise the letter from the sign. Sometimes there's no real connection. OK. Er... Let's do *M* and *N*. For *M* you put the middle three fingers of your right hand on the palm of your left hand. And *N* is very similar to that. But instead of putting three fingers on your left palm you just put two – that's the index finger and the middle finger.
Sam Kennedy:	So *M* is three, and *N* is two... Right.
Mandy Cooke:	Let's go on to *F*. For *F,* you put the index finger and the middle finger of your right hand on top of the index finger and the middle finger of your left hand.
Sam Kennedy:	Just a minute. Erm, index... middle... right... on top of index... middle... left... And they're at right angles to each other?
Mandy Cooke:	Yes. That's it.
Sam Kennedy:	OK.
Mandy Cooke:	For *G*, you put your right fist on top of your left fist.
Sam Kennedy:	Easy!
Mandy Cooke:	For *H*, you put your right palm against your left palm at right angles. Then, keeping your left hand still, you move your right hand up and across the fingers of your left hand.
Sam Kennedy:	There are some dotted lines and an arrow on the chart again.
Mandy Cooke:	That's right. For *O*, you put the tip of your right index finger against the tip of your left ring finger.
Sam Kennedy:	Right index... left ring... OK.
Mandy Cooke:	And for *S*, you put the little finger of your right hand against the little finger of your left hand.
Sam Kennedy:	Right little... against left little. At right angles?
Mandy Cooke:	At right angles? Yes! OK. Now we've just got two more to do: *W* and *Z*. But they're both quite difficult to describe. For *W*, you interlock the fingers of both hands.
Sam Kennedy;	That's the one that looks like a bunch of bananas.
Mandy Cooke:	That's it. And the last one... You put the fingertips of your right hand on the palm of your left hand and that's *Z*... OK?

SECTION 7 Agatha Christie ───────────────

Answers:

1 *b* 1890.
2 *d* 2,000,000,000
3 *b* was called *The Mysterious Affair at Styles.*
4 *b* used the pen-name Mary Westmacott.
5 *c* a famous archaeologist.
6 *b* *Postern of Fate.*

Interviewer:	On tonight's programme, we're going to look at the phenomenal success of the thriller writer, Agatha Christie, and with me is Kate Donaldson, author of a splendid new biography about the 'Queen

of Crime'. Kate, I suppose the first question is 'What's so special about Agatha Christie?'

Kate Donaldson: I think what interests me about her is that here you have a major literary figure who wrote 88 novels and 19 plays, whose work has been translated into 44 different languages with estimated sales of two billion books. And yet – in some ways – we know very little about her. She was an intensely private woman and there were certain things she would never talk about. She guarded her privacy like a tigress protecting her cubs. She never gave interviews and she would never comment on the gossip and scandal and rumour that surrounded her. And that makes her a compelling subject for a biographer...

Interviewer: So what facts do we know about her?

Kate Donaldson: Well, she was born in 1890 in Devon. Her father died when she was very young and she grew up with her sister and mother. By all accounts, it was a fairly strict childhood. In 1914, she married Archibald Christie, who was a colonel in the Royal Air Corps, and a few years later – in 1920 – there was the publication of her first novel, *The Mysterious Affair At Styles* – a book which introduced the public to one of her greatest characters, the Belgian detective, Hercule Poirot.. Well, this was the beginning of a very rich creative period. I think she did some of her best work in the next three or four years.

But then, one day in 1926, her husband called her into his study and announced that he'd fallen in love with another woman and he wanted a divorce.

Well, there then followed a bizarre sequence of events. Agatha got into her car and disappeared for six days. Nobody knows where she went or what she did. Some people say she tried to commit suicide, others suggest she went looking for the woman her husband wanted to marry. And when they eventually found her in a hotel in Yorkshire, she was in a terrible state: bruised, delirious, disorientated. She never explained what had happened to her during those six days. It remains a complete mystery – one of many, in fact...

Anyway, she was divorced in 1928, but two years later she married again. Her second husband was Max Mallowan, an archaeologist famous for his work in the Middle East. And from then on, she worked continuously for the next forty years.

Interviewer: And did she only write thrillers?

Kate Donaldson: No, there were also six romantic novels which she wrote under her pen-name Mary Westmacott, and an extraordinary autobiography which was finally published in 1978.

Interviewer: And was that the last book she wrote?

Kate Donaldson: No, her last book was *Postern of Fate*, although two novels which she had written in the 1940s, *Curtain: Poirot's Last Case* and *Sleeping Murder*, were published after her death in 1976.

Interviewer: And after all your research, Kate, are you any closer to understanding the real Agatha Christie?

Kate Donaldson: No, I don't think so, to be honest. As one French critic said, 'Agatha Christie's life was the greatest mystery story she ever wrote.' I think that's probably true and that's what makes her so interesting...

SECTION 8 The Radio Play

On the tape, there are fifteen sounds (ranging from dogs barking to a gate creaking open) which are the raw material for a number of new radio plays.

Divide the class into groups. Play the tape through two or three times and ask everyone to write down a description of what they hear. There may be some disagreement as to what the sounds are, but this is part of the exercise. Then ask the groups to create their own radio play by weaving narrative and dialogue around these fifteen sounds.

When giving the first public performance of their work some twenty minutes later, one member of the group should act as a narrator (setting the scene, linking the dialogue etc.) and the others should play one (or more) of the characters in the play. During the performance, the narrator operates the cassette machine, inserting the sounds into the play at the right moment. How long the plays are depends on how much dialogue and description is put between the sounds.

As with the Advertising Game on page 110, don't worry if this exercise begins slowly. The group will need to orientate themselves and work out what to do.

1 a tap dripping
2 footsteps
3 a knock on a door
4 a dog barking
5 a church bell ringing
6 a gate creaking open
7 laughter
8 a steam train pulling into a station
9 the sound of glass crashing
10 a dull thud
11 an owl hooting
12 a rustling of leaves and a twig cracked underfoot
13 a trumpet playing a few bars of music
14 applause
15 a helicopter taking off

SECTION 9 Blank filling

1 tell
2 been
3 the
4 called
5 has
6 of
7 come
8 are/feel
9 will/might/could
10 and/or
11 because/if/when
12 invites
13 if/whether
14 if/though/when
15 those/people
16 take
17 half/still
18 ages/hours
19 will
20 goes

SECTION 10 Word families

1 comedian
2 comic/comical
3 direction
4 director
5 unbelievably

6 believe
7 strengthen
8 spokeswoman/spokesman
9 speech
10 useless

SECTION 11 Phrasal verbs

1 Keep *off* the grass!
2 They kept *on* playing in spite of the rain.
3 You're walking too fast. I can't keep *up* with you!
4 Keep the noise *down!* I'm trying to get some sleep.
5 She wore three jumpers to keep *out* the cold.

SECTION 12 Phrasal verb story

Follow-up questions:

1 What did Karen Blackstone go through?
2 What did Frederick throw away?
3 Why did the bank carry out a survey?
4 Why does Karen Blackstone want to set up a charity division?
5 What suddenly dawned on Frederick?
6 Who had given up trying to work out what was going on?

SECTION I 'Yawning'

SECTION 2 Vocabulary multiple choice

1	*c*	go	**14**	*c*	a loan
2	*a*	up	**15**	*b*	alone
3	*c*	taking	**16**	*d*	lonely
4	*b*	look it up	**17**	*a*	a lawn
5	*c*	ripe	**18**	*d*	whole
6	*b*	wasp	**19**	*b*	boring
7	*c*	made	**20**	*b*	gossiping
8	*b*	up	**21**	*c*	down
9	*c*	I'm	**22**	*c*	far
10	*c*	stormed	**23**	*a*	sense
11	*a*	rained	**24**	*d*	needn't have
12	*b*	reigned	**25**	*d*	to taking
13	*d*	blew			

SECTION 3 Exam practice: Listening

Part 1 (6 marks)

1 true; **2** false; **3** true; **4** true; **5** false; **6** true; **7** true; **8** true; **9** false; **10** false; **11** false; **12** true.

(6 MARKS – ½ mark for each correct answer)

Newscaster: It's six o'clock on Monday 18th January and here is the news. There have been dramatic falls on stockmarkets around the world today following rumours that a major international bank may be on the verge of collapse. According to a report in this morning's *New York Times* the Pan National Finance and Loan Corporation is technically bankrupt and this has led to speculation that several financial institutions may be in similar difficulties.
Share prices have fallen in London, Paris, Frankfurt, Singapore, Tokyo and New York. The only stock exchange not affected was Hong Kong, which was closed for a public holiday.
In an attempt to steady equity markets, the G7 group of industrial nations are meeting for an emergency session in Vancouver and are expected to announce an immediate cut in interest rates.
On the London Metals Exchange, gold rose to $480 an ounce – its highest level for five years – but on other commodity markets, there were steep falls of between 15 and 18%. Hardest hit were prices for tea, coffee, wheat and sugar, which all slumped to record lows for the year.
A state of emergency has been declared on the Caribbean island of Barbados after Hurricane Sally hit the capital Georgetown early this morning. Official estimates put the extent of the damage at some £15,000,000 and hundreds of people have been left homeless.
Hurricane Sally is now heading north and is expected to reach Dominica and Guadeloupe in about two hours' time.

Unit 14

There has been a breakthrough in the fight against arthritis. Scientists at the Borodin University in Leningrad have announced the results of a three-year clinical trial on a new drug called Sedorafun. Writing in the latest edition of the medical magazine *The Lancet*, Professor Omlovsky – head of the research project – says that Sedorafun can slow down the onset of arthritis, fibrositis and rheumatism by up to 25%.

Football... In the Merseyside Derby, a late goal from Norman Whiteside gave Everton a 3–2 victory over League leaders, Liverpool... And in athletics, Sweden's Ole Jensen has set a new world record in the pole vault, with a clearance of 6 m 25 at the Grand Prix meeting in Geneva.

And finally the weather. Overnight, temperatures will fall to around 10°C (that's 50°F) and the outlook for tomorrow: cool and dry with long sunny periods and a high of 16°C (59°F).

Part 2 (6 marks) The cookery class

Answers:

1	flour	**6**	400	**11**	lemon juice
2	200	**7**	milk	**12**	raisins
3	butter	**8**	egg		
4	150	**9**	chopped bananas		
5	sugar	**10**	teaspoonful		

Cookery teacher:	So once you've collected all the ingredients together this is what you do...
	You put the flour in the bowl and then you add in 200g of butter, 150g of sugar, 400 ml of milk, an egg, two chopped bananas, a teaspoonful of lemon juice and some raisins... then you...

(fade)

Part 3 (8 marks) The garage

Answers:

1 *b* spark plugs.
2 *d* 4 years old.
3 *a* a bus.
4 *c* Thursday.

Mick Kanneck:	...And we're open from nine to eleven-thirty on Saturday morning, sir...Yes... Bye. Sorry to have kept you, Mr Jarvis. I was just on the phone to another customer. Right, now you're the Renault estate, aren't you? Just let me go over and get the work sheet, and we can go and take a look...
Karl Jarvis:	Was everything OK?
Mike Kanneck:	Oh yes. It's in quite good shape, considering the number of miles you do in a year. Now, just remind me. You've been having trouble with the electrics, haven't you?
Karl Jarvis:	Well, the engine keeps cutting out on me, especially first thing in the morning. And you know in my job – I'm a sales rep – you just can't

	afford to be off the road for any length of time. So I thought I'd better come and get it sorted out.
Mick Kanneck:	Yeah. Well, the problem was your spark plugs. They were completely worn out. When did you last change them?
Karl Jarvis:	I don't know... A couple of years ago, I suppose.
Mick Kanneck:	Well, there you are. No wonder you were having difficulties. Anyway, we took out the old ones and fitted you with a new set, and we've tried out the engine and it's fine now. Other than that, everything else was OK. Your brake pads were fine. So was your oil filter. We had a look at the exhaust pipe, tyres, fan belt, carburettor, distributor, battery, radiator. No problems at all. You've got a good little car there. How long is it that you've had it?
Karl Jarvis:	Three years now.
Mick Kanneck:	And did you buy it brand new?
Karl Jarvis:	No, it was a year old when I got it.
Mick Kanneck:	Ah, well, I tell you, for a four-year-old motor, it's in pretty good shape. As far as I can see, the only problem you've got now is this dent on the left-hand side. How did you get that?
Karl Jarvis:	I left the car on a double yellow line while I went in to see a client and when I got back, I found this parking ticket on the windscreen. Well, I was really angry, you know. I'd only been away for ten minutes... Anyway, I pulled out into the main road. I wasn't concentrating – I was still thinking about the ticket – and I suddenly saw this motorcycle messenger coming towards me... I swerved to avoid him and hit a bus coming down the bus lane...
Mick Kanneck:	So, do you want us to sort it out for you? You know, you might as well get it done while the car's here.
Karl Jarvis:	Well, that depends on how much it's going to cost.
Mick Kanneck:	Dents don't come cheap, Mr Jarvis. I don't know, about four hundred quid, I suppose – something like that. But it's hard to say... I mean, it could be less, it could be more. It also depends on how quickly you want it. We've got twenty-five vehicles in here at the moment. I can put you at the front of the queue, but I'd obviously have to charge you premium rates for that... You're looking at overtime, three men on the job rather than one, priority treatment. I'm saying four hundred quid but it could be more. But if I were you, I wouldn't go out on the road with a dent like that. It's not very safe.
Karl Jarvis:	Yeah. Oh, I suppose you're right. I'd better have it done. So how soon can you fix it for me?
Mick Kanneck:	Well... What day is it today? Tuesday, isn't it? I tell you what. I'll have it ready for you the day after tomorrow. And because it's you, I'll call it four hundred quid plus VAT and I won't charge you for the spark plugs...

SECTION 4 The Halifax Guide to Selling Your Home ——

SECTION 5 Exam practice: Paper 2 ————————

Add a set book question for number **5**.

SECTION 6 Exam practice

Paper 3

Word families

1 photographer
2 photographic
3 impressive
4 impressionable
5 hopeless
6 conclusion
7 bored
8 boring
9 totally
10 impolite

Papers 4 & 5

Explain that you will be playing the tape twice – and that students should write down headline summaries only, not every detail of the points made.

Interviewer: I'm joined by Jane Pitman again, and we're going to talk about Papers Four and Five. Jane, let's start with the Listening Comprehension. What advice would you give here?

Jane Pitman: Well, first, you must always read the instructions at the top of the exam paper. Make sure you understand exactly what you have to do. Secondly, try to read the questions or the written text before you hear the tape for the first time. Thirdly, don't panic if there are lots of words you don't know. These passages are never easy. You hear the native speakers talking at their normal speed and the subject is sometimes quite specific – something technical or detailed perhaps – so it may be difficult for you to pick up all the vocabulary. But don't worry. You don't have to understand every word. Fourthly, answer all the questions. You don't lose any marks if you make a mistake, so never leave an empty space. Fifthly, if you have a multiple choice comprehension and you're not sure of the answer, start off by eliminating the options that you know are definitely wrong. This makes your final choice much easier. And finally, when the tape is finished, check all your answers before the papers are collected. Check the spelling and the grammar and ask yourself the simple question, 'Do all my answers make sense?'

Interviewer: And what about the Interview, Paper 5?

Jane Pitman: Ah. Well, the first thing I would say here is, 'Be yourself.' Don't try to show off with long words or complicated expressions, just speak naturally and use simple, everyday language. Secondly, learn how to describe a photograph and make sure you know expressions like 'in the foreground', 'in the background', 'in the top left-hand corner', 'in the bottom right-hand corner', and so on.
The third point is if you get stuck, ask for help. For example, if there's a word you need for the picture and you don't know what it is, point to the photograph and say, 'I'm sorry. I've forgotten the English word for this,' or, 'What do you call this in English?'
Fourthly, at some point in the interview, the examiner will ask you a personal question about your hobbies, work, ambitions, interests or whatever. Make sure you prepare this kind of vocabulary well in advance. Fifth... If you have the time, read one of the set books and talk about it in the interview. And sixth, don't ... speak... too... quickly... Some people get very nervous intheexamandstarttalking sofastthattheexaminercan'tunderstandwhattheyaretryingtosay...

So, speak slowly, and if you're worried about pronunciation, remember that the more air you have in your lungs, the clearer your voice is. So practise taking deep breaths before you do the interview!

Group Interview Practice

There are two kinds of interview in Paper 5. Candidates can be tested either on a one-to-one basis or as part of a group.

In the one-to-one interview, the examiner asks the candidate:

    a to describe a photograph
    b to summarise a short text.

This is then followed by an open-ended discussion about either a theme raised by the picture or text, or the candidate's hobbies, interests, ambitions etc.

The group interview follows the format outlined on page 180 of the student's book.

• The *EFL General Handbook* referred to in the Introductory Notes gives extensive information about this part of the exam.

SECTION 7 *put*

1 It's getting dark. You'd better put *on* the light.
2 The waiter had dirty fingernails. It really put me *off* my food.
3 Is that the Town Hall? Can you put me *through* to extension 191, please.
4 Why do you always put me *down* in front of other people?
5 You're putting *on* weight. You should go on a diet.

SECTION 8 Phrasal verb story

Follow-up questions:

1 Lady Prescott drove through into the main prison square. What happened next?
2 How did Frederick feel when he got back to his cell?
3 Why was Frederick's escape hushed up?
4 What did they talk about at the Italian restaurant?

SECTION 1 'The Wedding'

SECTION 2 Vocabulary multiple choice

1	*b*	speak	14	*d*	overtaking
2	*d*	engaged	15	*a*	black
3	*a*	were	16	*b*	last
4	*a*	panic	17	*c*	truth
5	*a*	at the end of	18	*d*	sleepy
6	*c*	stomach	19	*a*	lie
7	*b*	favour	20	*b*	hear
8	*c*	leave	21	*c*	yet
9	*c*	mind	22	*d*	stung
10	*a*	comes out	23	*d*	candles
11	*b*	price	24	*a*	to
12	*c*	stairs	25	*b*	drop
13	*b*	much too			

SECTION 3 The Soap Opera

1 false; **2** true; **3** false; **4** true; **5** false; **6** true; **7** true; **8** true; **9** false; **10** false; **11** false.

My favourite soap is, er, *East Lather Street*, which is shown three times a week – that's every Monday, Wednesday and Friday. It's all about a group of people who live on a housing estate in Bath. The main characters are Dee Oderant, who runs the local cafe, Ayron Cupboard, who owns the dry cleaner's, and Anne Teseptic, who works in the chemist's. Now, the story's very simple. Dee Oderant's brother-in-law, Lou Brush, who used to be a roadsweeper before he found this bag of diamonds in a rubbish bin, is in love with Sue Ridge, who is the niece of Ayron Cupboard's best friend, Abe Lution. Now, although Lou Brush loves Sue Ridge, she's not interested in him because she's engaged to Des Infectant, the plumber who's just split up with Lorna Drett... Now, I suppose I'd better explain how all that happened because it was quite important. Lorna Drett, who's the step-daughter of Anne Teseptic's third cousin twice removed, had been going out with Des Infectant for a couple of years and then Des said that he wanted to play golf every Saturday with Abe Lution and Ayron Cupboard. That was a real problem because Lorna Drett hates sport. And so she gave Des an ultimatum. 'You're going to have to choose,' she said. 'It's either me or the golf!' Well, Des thought about it for a couple of minutes, picked up his golf clubs and walked off... And Lorna Drett got so angry that she went into the car park and went over to the mini cab that Abe Lution drives and broke all the windows. Now, Abe Lution, who was just standing there talking to Sue Ridge and Ayron Cupboard, went crazy and he told Lorna Drett that if she didn't give him the money to repair all the damage to his mini cab, he was going to take her to court. So, anyway, Lorna Drett is in a real state now. She's lost Des Infectant and she owes Abe Lution £250 and according to Lou Brush and Dee Oderant...

(fade)

SECTION 4 Differences

SECTION 5 Listening comprehension

Use the pause button at the end of each question.

1   If today is Monday, what day is it tomorrow?
2   If tomorrow is Wednesday, what day was it yesterday?
3   What is the shortest month of the year?
4   If this month is July, what is the month after next?
5   My watch, which is ten minutes slow, says one twenty-five. What is the actual time?
6   A plane takes off from Milan at ten past two in the afternoon. An hour and a half later, it lands in Paris. At what time does the plane arrive?
7   What do you get if you multiply 2.5 by 3?
8   What is a cricket?
9   What is a kingfisher?
10 When I go to work in the morning, I travel east. So what direction do I travel in when I come home again?

Answers:

1   *b*   Tuesday   (raise your left hand)
2   *a*   Monday   (raise your right hand)
3   *a*   February   (raise your right hand)
4   *d*   September   (stand up)
5   *a*   1.35   (raise your right hand)
6   *c*   15.40   (raise both hands)
7   *c*   7.50   (raise both hands)
8   *a*   an insect   (raise your right hand)
9   *a*   a bird   (raise your right hand)
10 **d**   west   (stand up)

SECTION 6 Linking the letters

SECTION 7 Humour

SECTION 8 Phrasal verb story

When the class have finished this final chapter of the story, ask some general, open-ended questions such as:

1   How did Frederick escape?
2   What happened after he crossed the road that links Oldtown to Newtown?
3   What happened in the lay-by?
4   Why did Lady Prescott leave Birmingham?
5   Describe the run-down area she grew up in.
6   Tell the story of Frederick and the kidney machines.
7   How did Frederick steal money from the bank?
8   Describe the conversation between Karen Blackstone and Frederick.
9   How did Lady Prescott smuggle Frederick back into the jail?
10 Describe the dinner in the Italian restaurant.

The Practice Test that follows has the same general format as the Cambridge First Certificate, but no course book can replicate the exact feel and tone of the original exam.

So, as I suggested in the introduction, you should encourage the class to do some of the original past papers published by UCLES and Cambridge University Press. I feel that there is no substitute for the genuine article and although a book like *Passport* can *prepare* your students for the exam, only authentic papers can really *test* them at the right level.

You may find these past papers:
a in book form: *Cambridge First Certificate Examination Practice I*

ISBN : 0 521 27427 3 (student's book)
ISBN : 0 521 27428 1 (teacher's book)
ISBN : 0 521 26264 X (set of 2 cassettes)

Cambridge First Certificate Examination Practice 2

ISBN : 0 521 33902 2 (student's book)
ISBN : 0 521 33903 0 (teacher's book)
ISBN : 0 521 32589 7 (set of 2 cassettes)

or

b as individual examination papers (available from UCLES at the address on page 8).

You may however like to use the Practice Test on pages 190 to 200 as a 'dry run' for the exam, doing each paper in class against the clock.

PAPER I Reading Comprehension

Section A

1	*b*	sentenced	14	*b*	far
2	*d*	spite	15	*c*	caught
3	*b*	arrive	16	*d*	China
4	*d*	far	17	*c*	lost
5	*c*	warden	18	*b*	off
6	*d*	lent	19	*d*	sprained
7	*c*	tell	20	*a*	match
8	*b*	had told	21	*a*	sew
9	*c*	held	22	*d*	use
10	*d*	slip	23	*a*	catch up with
11	*b*	effect	24	*c*	for
12	*c*	reach	25	*a*	blew out
13	*a*	ought			

Section B

FIRST PASSAGE

(from *As I Walked Out One Midsummer Morning* by Laurie Lee)

26 *a* had three brothers.
27 *d* had helped to pack his bag.
28 *c* a musical instrument.
29 *a* oppressive.
30 *c* had been thinking of leaving home for some time.

SECOND PASSAGE

31 *c* a brand of French fried chips.
32 *a* are made from various ingredients.
33 *d* send the empty pack back to the manufacturer.
34 *c* spread evenly over a grill pan.
35 *c* grilling is quicker than frying.

THIRD PASSAGE

(from *Bismarck* by A.J.P. Taylor)

36 *b* had a surprisingly high-pitched voice.
37 *d* sometimes wore a full beard.
38 *d* spent long periods on his own.
39 *c* was less self-confident than he seemed.
40 *a* managed to overcome his doubts.

PAPER 2 Composition

Add an appropriate set book question for number **5**.

PAPER 3 Use of English

Among the various possible answers for this section are:

1

1	before, after	**11**	had
2	at	**12**	too
3	at	**13**	a
4	to	**14**	in
5	few	**15**	take
6	into	**16**	so, incredibly
7	towards	**17**	up, over
8	like	**18**	first, second, other
9	hands	**19**	look, seem
10	to	**20**	whole, entire

2

1 He asked me what the time was.
2 You needn't have bought milk.
3 The last time I saw her was five years ago.
4 Andrew is younger than Mary.
  Andrew isn't as old as Mary.
5 If you hadn't arrived late, we would have caught the plane.
  If you had arrived on time, we wouldn't have missed the plane.
6 They had the painting valued by an art expert.
7 He is such a rude man that nobody likes him.
8 The warehouse was damaged by the fire.
9 I wish I hadn't resigned from that job.
10 Unless you pay me I won't finish the job.

3

1 Five people applied for the job.

2 I feel really guilty about what happened.
3 This dress is too long. Can you shorten it for me?
4 Just calm down. Don't be so aggressive.
5 £45.00 for a hamburger! That's absolutely ridiculous.
6 The advantages outweigh the disadvantages.
7 She's so unpredictable. You never know what she's going to do next.
8 We have considered your proposal very carefully.
9 I think you owe me an apology.
10 A government spokesman (spokeswoman) announced the news.

PAPER 4 Listening comprehension

First part

A court case

1 false; 2 true; 3 false; 4 true; 5 true; 6 true; 7 false; 8 true; 9 false;
10 true; 11 false; 12 false.

Barrister:	Your full name is Christine Theresa Sanderson?
Christine Sanderson:	Yes, that's right.
Barrister:	And you live at number 86, Park Street?
Christine Sanderson:	I do.
Barrister:	And you work as a senior security officer at Caxton Rutherford Press, a large printing firm in Broad Street?
Christine Sanderson:	That's correct.
Barrister:	Right. Now, Miss Sanderson... Would you tell the court how long you've been with the company?
Christine Sanderson:	Erm, I don't know exactly... Eighteen, perhaps twenty, years.
Barrister:	I see. And what is the nature of your work?
Christine Sanderson:	Well, Caxton Rutherford produce bank notes and share certificates from specially designed printing blocks. It's my job to keep those printing blocks safe and secure twenty-four hours a day seven days a week.
Barrister:	And where are these printing blocks normally kept?
Christine Sanderson:	In the main safe.
Barrister:	And where is that safe?
Christine Sanderson:	In room 159... On the fifth floor...
Barrister:	Now, Miss Sanderson, as a senior security officer with twenty years' service at the company, you had a key to that room, didn't you?
Christine Sanderson:	Yes. But...
Barrister:	And free, unrestricted access... You could be there on your own at any time. Day or night. No questions asked. No one had the right to challenge you... No one could stop you... You were able to come and go as you pleased... Isn't that right?
Christine Sanderson:	Yes, but I wasn't the only one... All the senior managers had keys. There were maybe a dozen people who had that kind of access to room 159.
Barrister:	But the other managers are not on trial for theft, embezzlement, forgery and laundering money, Miss Sanderson. You are.
Second Barrister:	Objection, m'lud.
Judge:	Sustained. Those last comments will be struck from the record.

	Mr Forsyth, you know the principles of this and other courts. Please show the defendant due respect, and conduct yourself with a little more restraint. This is a court of law, not a theatre.
Barrister:	I'm sorry, m'lud. Now, Miss Sanderson. When did you first meet Scott Thomas?
Christine Sanderson:	It was about a year ago when he placed a big order with Caxton Rutherford.
Barrister:	And how often have you met him since then?
Christine Sanderson:	Well, he comes to the printworks once or twice a month... We do quite a lot of work for his company now.
Barrister:	So, you have met him several times?
Christine Sanderson:	Yes...
Barrister:	And would you call him a close friend of yours?
Christine Sanderson:	No, not at all. He's just a business acquaintance, that's all...
Barrister:	A business acquaintance. I see... Right. Now let us come to the events of the 6th, 7th and 8th September last year... I understand that Mr Thomas visited the printworks on Thursday 6th September. Is that right?
Christine Sanderson:	Yes. He came in to check some documents.
Barrister:	And you met him on that day?
Christine Sanderson:	Yes, I did.
Barrister:	And then, one day later, on 7th September, you met him again, didn't you?
Christine Sanderson:	Yes... We had some business to discuss...
Barrister:	And where did this so-called 'business' meeting take place? In your office at the printworks, I suppose?
Christine Sanderson:	No... He invited me out to lunch.
Barrister:	To discuss business.
Christine Sanderson:	Yes...
Barrister:	At a restaurant five miles from the printworks.
Christine Sanderson:	Erm... yes...
Barrister:	And did you tell your secretary you were meeting Mr Thomas that day?
Christine Sanderson:	No...
Barrister:	And did you tell your boss, Mr Farraday, that you were meeting Mr Thomas that day?
Christine Sanderson:	No... I...
Barrister:	Indeed... Did you tell anyone at Caxton Rutherford that you were meeting Mr Thomas that day?
Christine Sanderson:	No, I didn't think it was necessary...
Barrister:	So on 7th September, you had a 'business' meeting which no one at your place of business knew anything about. Now, I am a fair and honest man, but that seems odd to me...
Second Barrister:	Objection, m'lud.
Judge:	Sustained. Please, Mr Forsyth...
Barrister:	My apologies, m'lud... Now, let us come to the crime itself. At sometime between midnight and 6am on Saturday 8th September, five printing blocks went missing from the safe in Room 159. Did you steal them, Miss Sanderson?
Christine Sanderson:	No, I didn't.
Barrister:	You're quite sure about that?
Christine Sanderson:	Yes.
Barrister:	I'm not... Now... moving forward a few hours... Can you tell the court what happened to you at 2pm on Saturday 8th, the very same day the safe was robbed?

Christine Sanderson:	I was arrested by the police.
Barrister:	And where were you at the time?
Christine Sanderson:	Cardiff Airport.
Barrister:	And what were you doing at Cardiff Airport?
Christine Sanderson:	I was just about to catch a flight to Madrid.
Barrister:	And the purpose of your visit?
Christine Sanderson:	I just needed a holiday... I'd been working very hard, and so I decided to take a few days off work... to go to Spain and get a bit of sun...
Barrister:	I see. And of course you had no idea that Scott Thomas – one of your business acquaintances – owned a flat in the centre of Madrid?
Christine Sanderson:	No, I didn't know that.
Barrister:	Miss Sanderson, do you recognise the blue suitcase over there? In the centre of the room...
Christine Sanderson:	Yes, I do.
Barrister:	Does it belong to you?
Christine Sanderson:	Yes.
Barrister:	And were you carrying that suitcase when they arrested you?
Christine Sanderson:	Yes, I was.
Barrister:	And what did the police find inside the suitcase?
Christine Sanderson:	Some printing blocks...
Barrister:	Yes, Miss Sanderson... Or to be more exact, the five printing blocks that had been stolen from the safe in room 159 just a few hours before... That's what you were carrying in the suitcase, wasn't it?
Christine Sanderson:	Yes... But I can explain everything...
Barrister:	Or perhaps I can explain it to you, Miss Sanderson? When you met Scott Thomas at the restaurant on Friday 7th September, he offered you a deal, didn't he? You were to steal five printing blocks and then take them to Madrid. He would produce £1,000,000 worth of bank notes and share certificates and then put you on a plane back to Cardiff. You would then drive to the Caxton Rutherford Press late on Sunday night, show your security pass at the main gate, let yourself into room 159 with your key and then put the printing blocks back into the safe. On Monday morning, the safe would be checked and everything would be in order. A simple plan, Miss Sanderson... Very clever... Very original... Caxton Rutherford would still have its printing blocks and Scott Thomas could lie low for a while and then flood the market with counterfeits and forgeries that would make you both rich. Mr Thomas was not just a business acquaintance, was he? He was your partner. You worked and planned and conspired together...
Christine Sanderson:	No, that's not true!
Barrister:	You were involved in an international counterfeiting operation centred on Madrid.
Christine Sanderson:	No... that's not true...
Barrister:	And over the previous twelve months, you'd lied and cheated and forged several documents... Hadn't you?
Christine Sanderson:	No, that's not true... It wasn't like that at all...

Second Part

The psychology of colour

1 strong or aggressive.

2 creative or intelligent.
3 kindness or gentleness.
4 an accountant or a lawyer.
5 white.
6 grey.
7 waiters.
8 brown.

Sue:	So, what happened?
Cathy:	What do you mean what happened?
Sue:	You know. When you asked Mr Murphy for a rise.
Cathy:	Oh... that... Erm. I changed my mind... I decided not to.
Sue:	What do you mean you decided not to? You told me that at nine o'clock this morning you were going to walk into his office, bang your fist on the table and demand an extra 15% a year, free health insurance, luncheon vouchers and a company car, and that if he didn't give you what you wanted, you were going to tear up your contract, hand in your resignation and leave the firm.
Cathy:	Ah... yes... well, I was going to do that, but, er, I didn't.
Sue:	Why? What happened?
Cathy:	You see, when I got into the office, I noticed that he was wearing a red shirt and red socks.
Sue:	So? What's that got to do with it?
Cathy:	Well... people who wear a lot of red are strong and aggressive, and you mustn't push them too far.
Sue:	Who told you that?
Cathy:	It's all in this book I'm reading called *Dealing With People – The Psychology of Colour* by Dr Michaela Hagena. She says that we use colour to establish our social identity, to send out signals to the world. You know, to tell people what kind of mood we're in. So when Mr Murphy decided to wear a red shirt and red socks this morning, he was saying to me – you know, subconsciously – 'Be careful, Cathy. I'm feeling strong and aggressive today. So don't ask me for a rise, because I won't give it to you.' So that's why I didn't say anything...
Sue:	Oh, that's a load of nonsense. And so what are you going to do now?
Cathy:	I'm going to wait until Monday.
Sue:	Monday? Why? What happens then?
Cathy:	Well, he always wears that purple tie on Monday, doesn't he?
Sue:	Yeah... So...?
Cathy:	Well, according to Dr Hagena, purple indicates kindness and gentleness. So when he wears the purple tie, he's saying to me – you know, subconsciously – 'Hello, Cathy. I'm in a good mood. Would you like a pay rise and a company car?'
Sue:	Oh, that's silly. Red socks... purple ties... I can't see the difference. It doesn't make any sense to me.
Cathy:	Ah, but that's where you're wrong, you see. It does make sense. Look, let me give you another example. Bathrooms.
Sue:	Yeah. What about them?
Cathy:	Well, according to chapter three – 'Bathrooms and Behaviour' – anyone who paints their bathroom yellow is creative and intelligent.
Sue:	Creative and intelligent! Pah... That's a load of rubbish. If you paint your bathroom yellow, all that means is that you like yellow bathrooms, nothing more, nothing less.
Cathy:	All right then. If you don't believe any of that, how about chapter

	four... 'Colours at Work'.
Sue:	Yeah. Go on...
Cathy:	Well, this is what she says on page 48: 'After twenty-five years of extensive scientific research, I can now tell you what colours you should wear at work.'
Sue:	Right. Go on.
Cathy:	And then she's got a list here, with all the details. I mean, let me give you some examples... The best colour for an accountant or lawyer is blue because blue means, 'Trust me,' 'I'm in charge,' 'I know what I'm doing.'
Sue:	And how do you know that?
Cathy:	Well, because it says so.
Sue:	OK. And what else?
Cathy:	Well... Bankers should never wear white. Dentists should never wear grey. Never trust a person who wears brown. And if you work as a waiter, always wear orange. This is good stuff... useful advice...
Sue:	Well, I tell you, I'm still not convinced. I don't believe a word of this. I mean, what about the yellow car I bought yesterday? You say that 'yellow' means 'creative and intelligent'. Are you telling me that my Renault is creative and intelligent?
Cathy:	Oh, no. It only applies to people, not things. But, well, just let me look up yellow cars in chapter nine, 'Motors and Motivation'... Let's just see what it says... Yes, here we are. Page 104. People who buy yellow cars are always bad-tempered...'
Sue:	Me? Bad-tempered? Just who does this Dr. Thingumy think she is, going round telling people they're bad-tempered? I'm not bad-tempered... I get really angry when I hear stupid comments like that. I mean, why doesn't she...?

(fade)

Third part

A mountain rescue

1   *d*   had ignored the advice of a local farmer.
2   *c*   very cold.
3   *a*   a young girl.
4   *c*   weather conditions are now getting better.

Nick Thomas:	Good morning. It's six o'clock on Thursday 9th November and here is the breakfast news from Radio Waverley. I'm Nick Thomas. Five climbers from the Ferriston Valley Mountaineering Club have been found safe and well after spending most of last night trapped in a cave on Ben Nevis. In the radio car, direct from the scene, here's Hana Jameson.
Hana Jameson:	Yes, good morning, Nick. I'm at the Glenroth Hospital where, a couple of hours ago, a Royal Air Force helicopter brought the five climbers. I can tell you that they are all safe and well. They're a bit cold and shaken but that's all... And I have with me Greg Anderson, the leader of the group... So, Mr Anderson, can you tell us what happened?
Greg Anderson:	Well... We were trying to get up the south-west face of Ben Nevis and in normal conditions they say it's quite a straightforward ascent. It's not very steep and there are plenty of tracks. Well, we'd been

climbing for about an hour or so, erm, without any problems – it was all routine – when all of a sudden, out of nowhere, this fog just descended. You know, like a blanket. And before we knew it, we just couldn't see a thing... Now we don't know the mountain very well. It was our first time up there. So there was no way we could get back. Erm... and we decided to look for some shelter... We managed to find a small cave with just enough room for the five of us, and so we got in there and settled down for the night. It was quite comfortable. We had a stove, sleeping bags, everything we needed... But then, about three o'clock this morning, there was a huge crash – an explosion like a bomb going off – and there was a rock fall that blocked off the entrance to the cave. Erm, we managed to shift some of the stones, but we couldn't get the entrance completely clear and, er, we started to panic a bit...

Hana Jameson: And so what did you do next?

Greg Anderson: Well, we had a small two-way radio, but it wasn't working. So we just stood at the front of the cave, shouting into the fog. Now, it turned out that we were about a hundred metres away from the place where the mountain ranger lives, and, erm, he has a ten-year old daughter who heard the noise. Anyway, she had the presence of mind to raise the alarm. She woke up her father and that was it... Twenty minutes later, there was a search party up on the ridge and they got us out and, erm, gave us a cup of soup and, erm, flew us down to the hospital...

Hana Jameson: Now, the Ben Nevis area is well known for its sudden changes of weather – it's unpredictable climate. Did nobody tell you about this before you set out?

Greg Anderson: Well, yes, to be honest. We were a bit stupid really, because, erm, the farmer down at Oakwood, he warned us there could be trouble. You know, with the fog... Apparently yesterday afternoon, his animals had started acting strangely. They were all lethargic and listless. They just wanted to sleep, and, erm, they've got a saying, in this part of the world that, 'when the cat is not chased by the dog, on Ben Nevis there's going to be fog.' But when the farmer told us this 'story', I just thought it was a bit of a joke. And I didn't believe him... And so we went on up the mountain regardless. The weather was fine. It was dry. There wasn't a cloud in the sky. And I mean, although it was freezing cold, you never expect something to go wrong. You just take a risk, don't you? And, erm, sometimes it doesn't work out...

Hana Jameson: And what are weather conditions like now, up in the mountains?

Greg Anderson: Well, I've just been on the phone to the rescue services. I wanted to thank them for everything they did for us. And they said the fog is clearing. It's much better than it was when they brought us down in the helicopter. The wind's picking up and it's going to be a good, clear, sunny day up there...

Hana Jameson: Just right for climbing?

Greg Anderson: Well, yes... But not for us – not yet anyway...

Hana Jameson: And so, with the news that the five climbers from the Ferriston Valley Mountaineering Club missing overnight are now safe and well, this is Hana Jameson, at the Glenroth Hospital, handing you back to the studio...

PAPER 5 Interview

To practise the one-to-one interview, divide the class into pairs and ask the students to consider the two sets of questions on page 200.

For the group interview, go through the notes on page 179 and then, when the procedure is clear, ask the class to do the exercise on page 201 – interpreting the four passages, discussing the follow-up questions and doing the creative free-form question about the new television station, TV-9.

Group Dictation

Divide the class into groups of four sitting in the NEWS format described on page 10 of the Introductory Notes and write the numbers 1 to 5 up on the board.

Explain that you are going to play the same passage five times and that you would like everyone in the group to write down word for word what they hear. The idea is that by the end of the fifth playing, each member of the group should have his or her verbatim copy of the text.

With the tape playing at normal speed, it's almost impossible to pick up every word and detail so encourage the group to pool information and ideas.

Each time you play the tape, cross out one of the numbers on the board.

a Play the tape.
b Give the group two or three minutes to work out an approach to the task.
c Play the tape a second time.
d Give the group three or four minutes to compare notes.
e Play the tape a third time.
f Give the group four or five minutes to compare notes.
g Play the tape a fourth time.
h Give the group four or five minutes to compare notes.
i Play the tape a fifth time.
j Give the group four or five minutes to compare notes.

In theory, everyone should now have their own version of the story. Ask one person to read out what they have written. Invite the class to interrupt if they hear any mistakes.

One variation on this exercise is for you to read the passage yourself instead of playing the tape. This has one big advantage in that you can alter the pace at which the group hear the text, perhaps reading the passage slower the second and third time round.

At midday on Tuesday 4th November, three men walked into the London branch of the International Credit Bank. As soon as they were inside the building, they opened their jackets and took out silver pistols. They ran to the centre of the room and began shouting.

'The guns are loaded and and this is a raid,' they screamed. 'Just do what we tell you and no one will get hurt.'

The first robber aimed his pistol at the ceiling and fired a warning shot. Then he turned towards the twenty or so customers who had been standing in a queue. 'Lie down and put your hands behind your head,' he shouted.'Don't try to be a hero. Just keep still and do exactly what you're told.' The second robber ran forward and pointed a gun at one of the cashiers. He threw a bag under the glass window and began giving instructions. 'Take the bag,' he said. 'Fill it with cash. I want all the fifty pound notes you've got. And get on with it.'

The cashier nodded, filled the bag and then raised her arms above her head.

The third robber stood in the centre of the room. 'Where's the manager?' he shouted. 'I want the manager!' A tall woman came forward. 'What do you want?' she asked.

'The safe,' the robber said. 'I want you to get the key and open the safe. And hurry it up.'

The manager walked across the room and opened a small, red cupboard. She took out a key and moved towards the back of the building. 'Are you sure you want me to open the safe?' she asked. 'Get on with it and stop asking questions,' the third robber shouted. The manager put the key in the lock and then turned a white handle.

'Now open it!' the man said.

'If you insist,' the manager replied. She pulled open the door of the safe. A dozen lights flashed on the far wall and the alarm bells began to ring. The third robber raised his gun and pointed it at the manager...